ON TO STALINGRAD

DIE WEHRMACHT IM KAMPF

ON TO STALINGRAD

Operation *Winter Thunderstorm* and the attempt to relieve
Sixth Army, December 1942

HORST SCHEIBERT

Translated by
JANICE W. ANCKER

Series editor:
MATTHIAS STROHN

CASEMATE
Philadelphia & Oxford

AN AUSA BOOK
Association of the United States Army
2425 Wilson Boulevard, Arlington, Virginia, 22201, USA

Published in the United States of America and Great Britain in 2021 by
CASEMATE PUBLISHERS
1950 Lawrence Road, Havertown, PA 19083, USA
and
The Old Music Hall, 106–108 Cowley Road, Oxford OX4 1JE, UK

Originally published as Die Wehrmacht im Kampf 10: Horst Scheibert, *Nach Stalingrad—48 Kilometer! Der Entsatzvorstoss Der 6.Panzerdivision Dezember 1942* (Heidelberg: Kurt Vowinckel Verlag, 1956)

Hardback Edition: ISBN 978-1-61200-806-6
Digital Edition: ISBN 978-1-61200-807-3

A CIP record for this book is available from the British Library

Printed and bound in the United States of America by Integrated Books International
Typeset in India by Lapiz Digital Services, Chennai.

For a complete list of Casemate titles, please contact:

CASEMATE PUBLISHERS (U.S.)
Telephone (610) 853-9131
Fax (610) 853-9146
Email: casemate@casematepublishers.com
www.casematepublishers.com

CASEMATE PUBLISHERS (UK)
Telephone (01865) 241249
Email: casemate-uk@casematepublishers.co.uk
www.casematepublishers.co.uk

Front cover: Panzers crossing the bridge over the River Don near Stalingrad, December 1942. (Bundesarchiv, Bild 101I-218-0544-18)

Contents

Translator's note

I wish to thank my husband, Clinton J. Ancker, III, Col, Ret. for his enormous help on this translation. I am in awe of his expertise and am finally truly grateful for all those military books he has collected.

Janice W. Ancker

Foreword

Stalingrad. The name of the industrial city on the Volga will be connected forever with the cataclysmic battle that was fought here between August 1942 and February 1943, and which led to the destruction of the German Sixth Army in the ruins of the city that bore Stalin's name. The events of the battle within the pocket are well known and have been thoroughly studied, not least the gruesome details of human suffering on both sides. One episode in this struggle is, however, less known and understood; in fact, this chapter is often mentioned only in passing when the battle of Stalingrad is discussed. This is the German relief attempt, which saw a German Panzer Korps fight its way towards the encircled Sixth Army.

This operation, called *Wintergewitter*, or *Winter Thunderstorm*, was facing problems from the start. The Germans were not able to assemble the envisaged force of four divisions, and, in the end, the attack was launched on 12 December 1942 by only two divisions, the 6th and 23rd Panzer Divisions. During the operation, some reinforcements arrived, in particular the 17th Panzer Division, but the odds were against the Germans from the start. The Soviets realised the threat that this relief operation posed and threw large quantities of troops against the German LVII Panzer Korps. As a consequence, the German advance was slow and costly, but the German troops continued to fight their way towards the encircled troops in Stalingrad. However, by 24 December 1942, the troops were exhausted and Soviet counterattacks forced the Germans to abandon the offensive. This sealed the fate of the soldiers in Stalingrad. The encircled troops had been able to hear the fighting of the advancing relief forces and their clashes with the Soviets. Over the Christmas period, they noticed that the sound of battle faded and they realised that the relief attempt had failed. This was a bitter Christmas present for the encircled troops, who understood that this meant the end of the Sixth Army. The relief force was stopped approximately 48 kilometres short of the pocket. At this stage, the only chance of survival for at least a part of the encircled troops would have been the attempt to break through to the relief force. This order never came. The consequences were bitter for the soldiers in Stalingrad. The exact casualty figures are not known, but it is fair to assume that approximately 100,000 men died in the pocket; 90,000 went into captivity and only 5,000 returned home. The Soviets suffered even higher casualties in this tragic episode of World War II.

This book, first published in German in 1956, tells the story of the relief attempt. The author, Horst Scheibert, served as a company commander in one of the tank companies of 6th Panzer Division as it was fighting its way towards the perimeter of the Stalingrad pocket. He continued to fight in the Wehrmacht after the relief attempt had failed, and, by the end of the war, he had been highly decorated, including both classes of the Iron Cross and the German Cross in Gold. After World War II, he joined the West-German Bundeswehr and reached the rank of Brigadier. Combining the reports in war diaries and other official communications with his own personal experience, the author creates a vivid picture of the struggles as the division desperately tried to fight its way to the perimeter of the Stalingrad pocket. The fighting was hard. As Scheibert states in the introduction, his regiment lost seven out of eight tank company commanders in December 1942. Only Scheibert escaped unscathed. It is this combination of different perspectives that makes the book particularly valuable, and which offers new insights into this less well-known episode of one of the most gruesome struggles in the history of warfare.

Prof. Matthias Strohn, M.St., DPhil., FRHistS
Head of Historical Analysis, Centre for Historical Analysis and
Conflict Research, Camberley
Visiting Professor of Military Studies, University of Buckingham

Glossary of Rank Equivalents

German	English
General der Infanterie	General of the Infantry
General der Panzertruppe	General of Armored Troops
Generalleutnant	Lieutenant-General
Oberst	Colonel
Oberstleutnant	Lieutenant-Colonel
Major	Major
Hauptmann	Captain
Oberleutnant	First Lieutenant
Leutnant	Lieutenant
Stabsfeldwebel	Staff Sergeant
Oberfeldwebel	First Sergeant
Feldwebel	Sergeant
Unteroffizier	Corporal
Obergefreiter	Lance Corporal

Editor's Note: *These are only approximate equivalents as some German ranks have no real equivalent in English-speaking armies.*

Maps

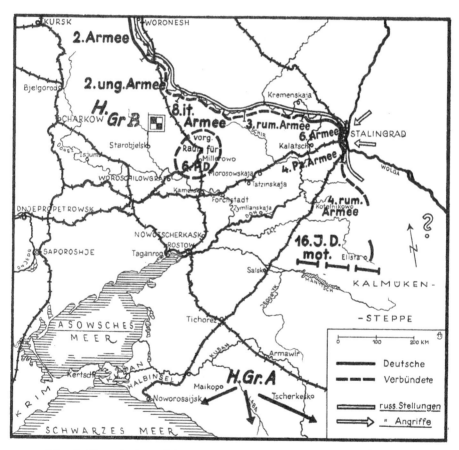

Map 1: Organisation of the German south flank, mid-November 1942.

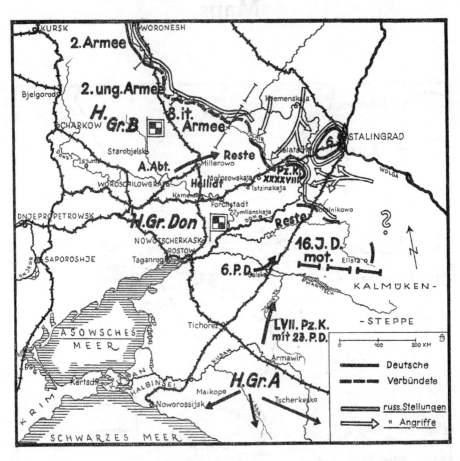

Map 2: Situation of the newly formed Army Group Don, end of November 1942.

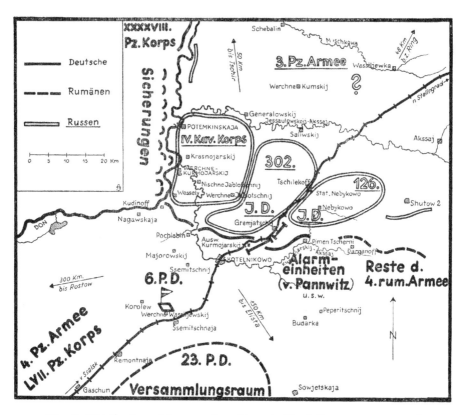

Map 3: Distribution of forces and positions in Kotelnikovo, on or around 2 December 1942.

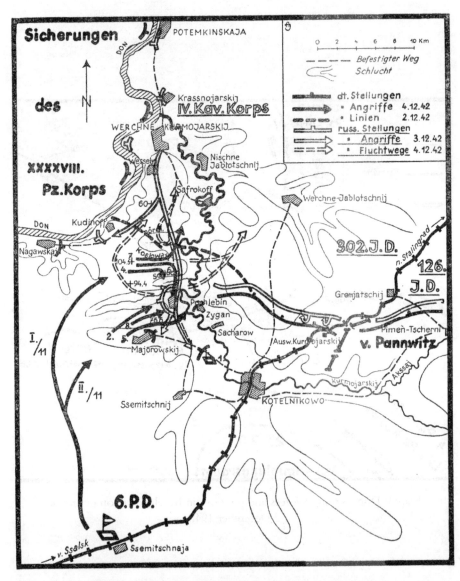

Map 4: The battles for Pokhlebin, 3–4 December 1942.

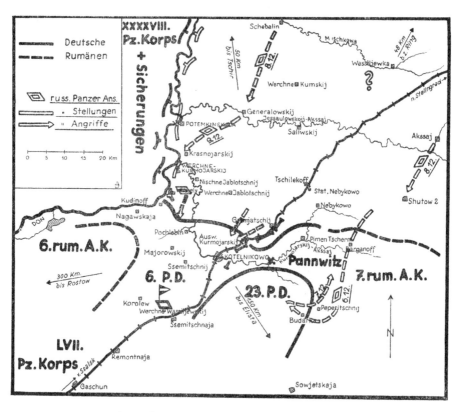

Map 5: Battles and movements prior to the beginning of the attack,
6–11 December 1942.

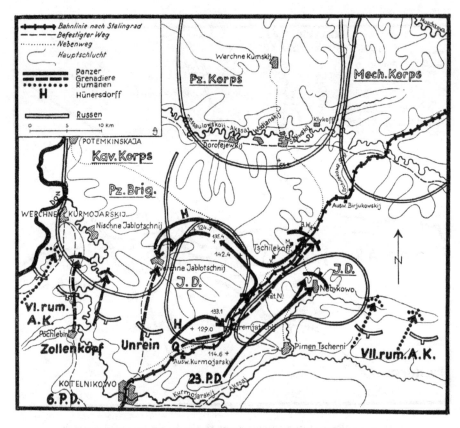

Map 6: The breakthrough, 12 December 1942.

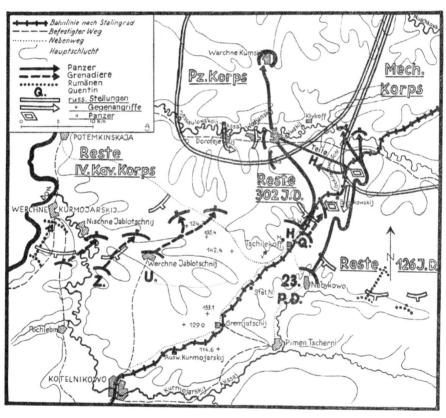

Map 7: The advance to Aksai positions, 13 December 1942.

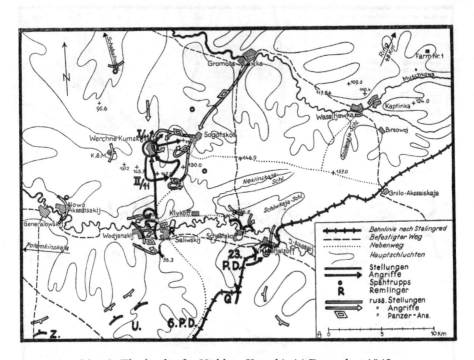

Map 8: The battles for Verkhne Kumski, 14 December 1942.

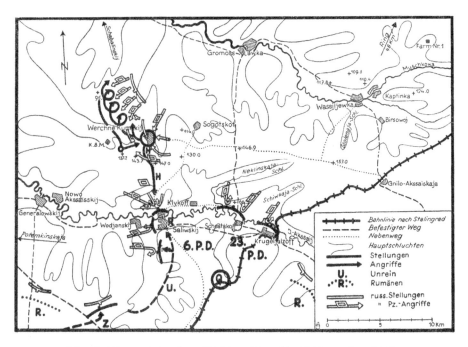

Map 9: The tank battle at Verkhne Kumski, 15 December 1942.

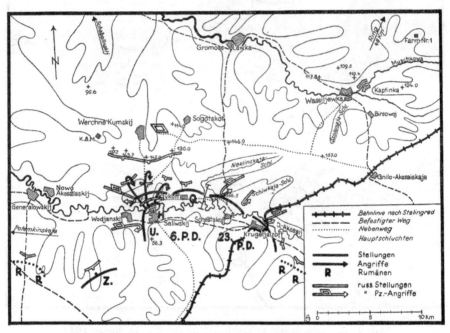

Map 10: The fortification of the Aksai Front, 16 December 1942.

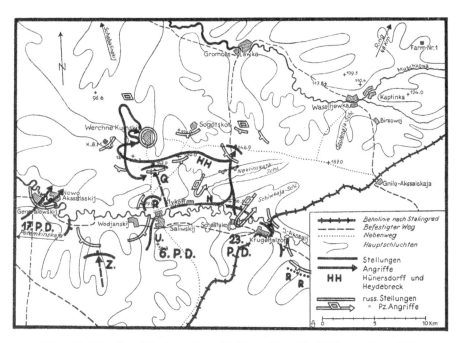

Map 11: The first failed attack on Verkhne Kumski, 17 December 1942.

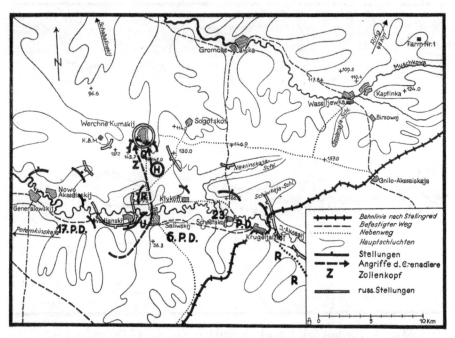

Map 12: The second failed attack on Verkhne Kumski, 18 December 1942.

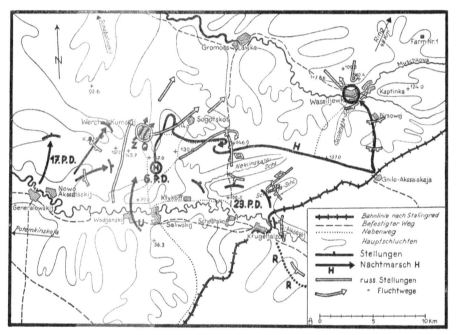

Map 13: The breakthrough at Vassilyevska, 19 December 1942.

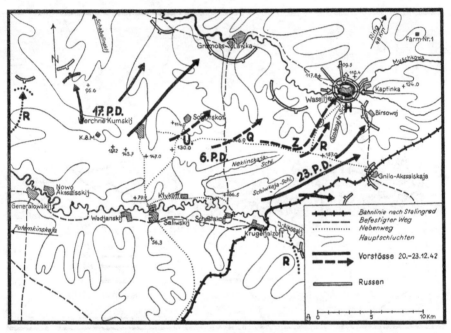

Map 14: The push to the Myshkova by LVII Panzer Corps, 20 December 1942.

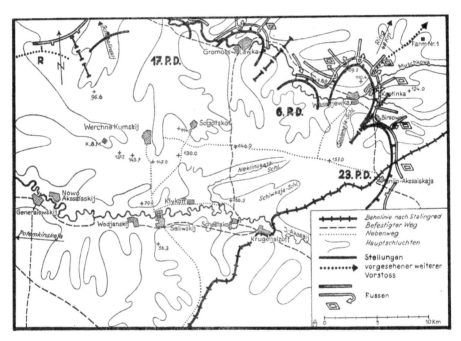

Map 15: The final positions before breaking off the attack, 23 December 1942.

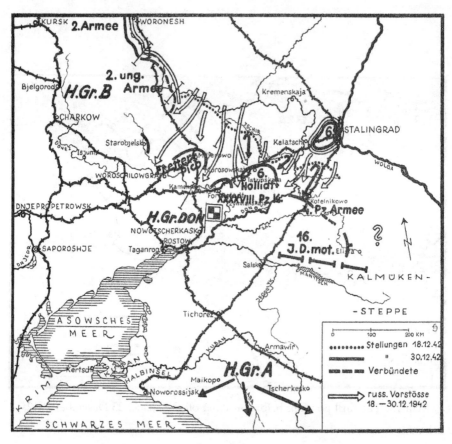

Map 16: Situation after the collapse of the Italian Eighth Army, end of December 1942.

The circumstances proved stronger than our firm resolve to liberate you.

Introduction

In his book *Verlorene Siege* (*Lost Victories*), Generalfeldmarschall Erich von Manstein writes:[1]

> ... This life and death race, which began with the 12 December appearance of the Fourth Panzer Army to relieve the Sixth Army, can only be drawn here in broad strokes. It is impossible to describe the lightning-quick shift in circumstances that the LVII Panzer Corps faced, with an enemy who continuously threw new forces into the battle – tanks above all. The agility of our panzer commanders and the superiority of our panzer crews stood the test brilliantly during this time, as did the bravery of the panzer grenadiers and the ingenuity of our anti-tank defence. At the same time, however, it also demonstrated what an old, tried and true panzer division such as the 6th could accomplish in battle when fully equipped with panzers and assault weapons, and while under the superb command of General Raus and the panzer commander Oberst von Hünersdorff (who would unfortunately die in battle later, while at the vanguard of this division) ...

The task of the present volume is to represent as clearly as possible the situation described in the above statement:

> ... it is not possible to describe the quick as lightning shift of circumstances in the battles of the LVII Panzer Corps ...

In doing so, I hope to rescue from oblivion these difficult campaigns which were so momentous in their goals, tragic in their outcome, but rich in lessons learned.

If this narrative relies heavily on the perspective of the 6th Panzer Division, it is because at one point in time, this division, which was in the middle of the LVII Panzer Corps, had to shoulder the main burden of the battles. Moreover, thanks to its strengths, it helped support its neighbours who were weaker in materiel. In addition, the author himself was a member of this division, serving as commander of a panzer company in Battle Group Hünersdorff, a key player, and participated in all the battles during that period. Lastly, for a certain time, the only original data sources from that period were from this division.

The publications thus far on the attempt to relieve Stalingrad are almost all tarnished by inaccuracies as to time, locations, and numbers. There are also distortions, both intentional and unintentional, as well as exaggerated and embroidered versions of events. Relying as it does on a large number of documents, this book places particular emphasis on objectivity.

A further reason for the scarcity of factual reporting thus far may also lie in the fact that the operation stood under the shadow of the Stalingrad situation itself. Of the officers involved, a great many were killed in this, and in later battles, or were wounded and sidelined early on. From the 11th Panzer Regiment of the 6th Panzer Division, for instance, after just one month of deployment (from 3 December 1942 on), out of the eight combat company commanders, only this author was still available for duty. For the other units, it was not much different. This fact explains why, until now, only the former members of the higher leadership staffs or outside observers have written on this subject. Even with the best of intentions, particularly for the latter group, it was naturally impossible to provide them with objective and precise descriptions from a military science perspective.

In the spelling of the place names, it must be noted that at that time a variety of map materials were available (on the German side 1:100,000 and 1:300,000; on the Russian side 1:200,000). All editions provide designations in modified spellings. Except citations from reproductions of captured Russian orders and other sources, efforts were made to synchronise all the designations that appear in this book. The time designations on the German side are given in Central European time, so that due to the distances involved, the local time will be two hours later.

Without the generous help (providing details, reports, and documents) of many participants of the battles at that time, especially the former

Hauptmann [captain] and adjutant of Battle Group Hünersdorff, Helmut Ritgen, it would not have been possible to complete this compilation. I wish to take this opportunity to express my gratitude for all their help.

Weilburg/Lahn, 31 December 1955   *Horst Scheibert*

CHAPTER I

Advance, Objectives, and Initial Situation

End of November to Beginning of December 1942 (Maps 1 and 2)

Equipment and battle strength of the 6th Panzer Division
Transport from Brittany to the Kalmyk Steppe
The Southern Front (mid-November)
The battles beginning on 19 November 1942, both sides of Stalingrad

In May 1942, after the hard winter battles of 1941–2 in the Moscow area, the 6th Panzer Division was transferred to France (Brittany) for rest and replenishment.

The 11th Panzer Regiment, previously supplied with equipment such as the Skoda 35 (t), was to receive new German weapons and vehicles. Although in previous deployments (Poland, France, the Baltics, Leningrad, and Moscow) the Skoda panzers had proven excellent, members of the regiment looked forward to the new German models, in great measure because during the previous deployments it had grown clear that the Skoda, with its 3.7cm cannons, was no match for the Russian T34 and the KVI and II, which were seen more and more often.

Unfortunately, these hopes were dashed. In place of the all-terrain wheeled vehicles so desperately desired (especially in the supply area), the regiment received more conventional motor vehicles, which came in a myriad of models, with problems such as weak engines and axles. In future deployments the equipment situation would become not only problematic, but often critical. The same was true of tractors, one of the few vehicles of German manufacture actually useable in the eastern deployment, but whose distribution was inadequate.

The equipment inventory for the 11th Panzer Regiment was in accord with the *War Strength Table of Organisation 1103*.[i] It consisted of 21 Panzer IIs (2cm cannon, long), 75 Panzer IIIs (5cm cannons, long), 30 Panzer IIIs (7.5cm cannon, short), 24 Panzer IVs (7.5cm cannons, long), and nine armoured command post vehicles.[ii] With this, the division now owned over 160 panzers, compared with its previous inventory of only 200 Skodas [which were less powerful]. This difference in numbers arose from the consolidation of three battalions into two during the process of the restructuring.

Further, the staff of the 6th Rifle Brigade disappeared. The 4th and 114th Rifle Regiments were re-designated as panzer grenadier regiments. The 57th Reconnaissance Battalion and the 6th Motorcycle Rifle Battalion (*Kradschütz 6*) were consolidated into the 6th Reconnaissance Battalion, but the nickname 'K6' still held on for some time.[iii]

In the effort to strengthen armour, II Battalion/114th Panzer Grenadier Regiment received SPWs (*Schützenpanzerwagen*) for troop transport, as well as I Battalion/76th Artillery Regiment, and one company of self-propelled gun carriages from the 41st Panzerjäger Battalion.[iv] These last three formations, along with parts of the now stronger armoured combat engineers (57th Pioneer Battalion) and the panzer regiment, were intended to represent the armoured component within the division. All exercises and war games were based on this.[v]

---

i   *Kriegsstärkenachweis* = K.St.N. 1103

ii Translator's note: most of these vehicles came in two variations, the first with a short-barrelled cannon, and later models with the longer barrel. The longer barrel gave higher velocity and greater effect than the short barrel.

iii The author or the radio messages often, confusingly, refer to 'K-6'. To prevent confusion, this translation will use 6th Reconnaissance Battalion in lieu of 'K-6.'

iv Translator's note: SPW = *Schützenpanzerwagen* = armoured infantry carrier. This is most similar to the American half-track. See F. M. von Senger und Etterlin, *German Tanks of World War II*, Stackpole Books 1969, Plate #144 in Illustrated Section. This translation will use SPW.

v   57th Pioneer Battalion was an engineer battalion.

At first glance, the division now appeared stronger than before. But at regimental level, this was not the case, especially when compared to the enemy, whose equipment had been strengthened in the meantime. Apart from the smaller number of German troops, the German panzer models proved to be a poor match for the Russian ones. The German Panzer II and III (7.5cm, short) were intended to be deployed primarily against the enemy's infantry troops, and when deployed against the T34, the Panzer III (5cm, long) was only effective at 800m or closer. The Russian T34, on the other hand, could destroy every panzer model present in the regiment, hitting from as great a distance as 1,500m. The penetration power of the Russian 7.62cm cannon (T34) was met or exceeded only by the German 7.5cm long, and naturally, the well-known 8.8cm anti-aircraft gun (*Flak*).[vi] These two stronger weapons, however, were available in only relatively small numbers, in the anti-tank units [*Panzerjäger*], designated anti-aircraft units, and the panzer regiment, with its 24 Panzer IVs.

Assuming that in a longer deployment, the number of panzers facing the enemy quickly decreases and then levels off to about one third of the starting inventory, not many weapons remained with sufficient power to challenge the enemy.

Despite this, after the months-long infantry deployments of the previous winter in the outskirts of Moscow, and after the loss of almost all vehicles, the division was quite pleased to finally receive the weapons they had been deprived of for so long. Along with rest and recovery in Brittany (visits home and excursions to the Atlantic and Channel coasts), field exercises were carried out with enthusiasm and a desire to gain confidence with the new equipment and to orient their replacements in their new tasks.

The division originated in Rhineland and Westfalia and recruited there. The Westphalians had outstanding soldierly qualities: the Rhinelanders brought mobility, while the men of the Ruhr offered mechanical expertise, which made up an impressive complement of talents. In previous deployments, the division had experienced substantial victories, and thanks to

---

vi   British and American nomenclature uses millimetres (e.g. 76.2mm cannon).

good leadership, casualties remained within a tolerable range. This meant that, along with the irreplaceable older lance corporals (*Obergefreiten*), there was still a good stock of NCOs and officers. These were men who had sweated together through many of the same deployments, had experienced combat, and were filled with esprit. From this perspective, the level of combat power could be characterised as excellent. Every soldier felt far superior to his Russian counterpart, had confidence in his weapons, and confidence in his well-trained leaders. Particularly in the panzer regiment there existed a relationship between all service ranks that was rich in trust and shared destiny. They fought as one team.

The division commander, Generalmajor Raus, like all regimental and battalion or detachment commanders, came up through the division and enjoyed the complete trust of all soldiers.[vii] A few months prior to the first deployment of the 11th Panzer Regiment, the regimental commander, Oberst R. Koll, was transferred to a different area of responsibility in the OKH (*Oberkommando des Heeres* = Army High Command), which caused no small amount of grief. But the new commander, Oberst von Hünersdorff, soon proved to be a fully effective replacement, particularly later in the deployment. The entire division now faced its new mission with confidence.

By the end of October 1942, there were ever-growing hints that the pleasant time in Brittany was about to end. After the landing of the Americans in North Africa, there were hopes of being sent to occupy southern France. Such hopes soon proved false. Winter gear for both vehicles and men came rolling in, and by the beginning of November the first embarkations for the eastern front began.

The train route began in a sweep around Paris, then continued diagonally through western Germany, through part of Berlin, and further on to the east. At the Oder river, the first snow appeared. Their stated destination was southern Russia, and their mission was to assemble behind the long front held by allies (Romanians, Italians, and Hungarians). Because there were no deployment orders yet, the division was to remain in the area between the Don and Donez in the approximate area of Millerovo, as army group reserve.

---

vii *Abteilung* = battalion or detachment, depending on context.

Baranoviche. Here began White Russia and with it, partisan territory. Destroyed locomotives and wagons were clearly visible on both sides of the train track, signs of the partisan warfare that had been waged here. All the way through the gigantic forest regions to Gomel, route security was strengthened. As a safeguard against mines, a wagon carrying sand travelled in front of the locomotive engine. Briansk lay in deep snow. Further along from Kursk to Byelgorod, the terrain opened up and we entered Ukraine, with its steppe stretching to the south and east.

The news from Stalingrad dominated our conversations. Despite a lack of clarity in the earliest reports, it was clear that since 21 November, a large number of troops had been surrounded, and that outside of this *Kessel*, or pocket, the battles continued. To the officers it seemed quite certain that we would be deployed there sooner or later.

At Kharkov, we had to cross the Donez river in order to reach the area of Millerovo. For most of the division, the trip south toward the area of the Donez continued at an increased tempo. At Rostov we crossed the Don, continued further south near Salsk and turned off to the north-east toward Stalingrad. From the opposite direction came trains with the wounded, and members of our division who first encountered them passed on the news of fighting at Kotelnikovo. There was no longer any question about where the entire division would be deployed.

As the journey continued, we moved more and more slowly, and the trains sometimes moved within visual distance of each other. The transports from Brittany to this region took 18 to 20 days' travel, and every man longed for the journey's end. Only someone who had experienced transport with eight men in one section, with a perpetually stinking stove, constant freezing temperatures, never being properly washed, and never being able to stretch out – all of this for a period of 450 hours – could ever comprehend the term 'transport rage' (*Transportkoller*).

At the start of December, the first panzer transports unloaded about 30km south-west of Kotelnikovo. They would not be given a long rest.

The following overview of the previous days' events on the Don may provide a better understanding of what we faced.

In mid-November of 1942, after the summer offensive, the southern flank of the German Army East lay as follows:

Army Group A was in the Caucasus with its right flank at the Black Sea; its left flank, however, became lost in the steppe south of Elista, never having reached the Caspian Sea.

Russian resistance was hardening to the same degree as the Germans', with both suffering the effects of the enormous distances, shortages in fuel, ammunition, and all types of supplies.

Far to the north in the area of Stalingrad, a second, very strong assembly of German forces (the Sixth Army and Fourth Panzer Army) was engaged in intense battles with the Russians, who were throwing increasing numbers into those fights. In the Kalmyk steppe, between these two groups, stood the Romanian Fourth Army (front length about 250km!), which had almost no contact with the one-and-only backup unit, the German 16th Infantry Division (motorised) at Elista.

On a 600km-long front north-west of Stalingrad, adjoined to the Italian Eighth Army and the Hungarian Second Army, was the Romanian Third Army. This front stretched from the upper corner of the larger bend of the Don, almost to Voronezh. Not until Voronezh were German units joined with them along this front. Positioned behind the allied armies were only a few reserves, but actually with no strong German troop units. This line was known to be dangerously weak.

Army Group B, which manned the stretch from Elista to Voronezh, often pointed out this hazardous situation to higher-ups, but sufficient measures were never taken.

The weakness of these allied armies offered the Russians the chance to cut off Stalingrad directly.

And on 19 November 1942, that is just what happened. The Russian forces, each with an assault army reinforced by masses of tanks, came at Stalingrad from the north and south. Within 48 hours they defeated the weak Romanian resistance and closed the ring around Stalingrad.

It would be unjust to shift the blame for this onto the Romanians. Unlike the Italians and Hungarians, whose lines ultimately crumbled, they fought with superb bravery, but neither in terms of equipment, strength, nor leadership were they a match for the Russian onslaught. The mistake lay in the basic approach to the summer operations by the OKW (*Oberkommando der Wehrmacht* = Armed Forces High Command).

It attempted to achieve too much all at the same time, with forces that were too weak. Later on, they assigned the allies a sector of the front that was too important and too long. By this time, it had become Hitler's obsession to capture the city that bore the name of his greatest adversary – at any cost. Therefore, the OKW ordered Army Group B – in an incredibly ignorant assessment of the enemy – to throw all its units into the all-consuming battle for the city of Stalingrad. Although risk-taking does involve pushing limits, the limits here were greatly exceeded. After having failed to take the city in the first onslaught, there should never have been this kind of concentration of forces on such an exposed position.

The northward attack by the Russians took place from a rather large bridgehead that remained available to them at the upper bend of the River Don. After breaking through the Romanian Third Army, the Russians rolled their tank corps toward the south and south-east, and soon reached the most important resupply railway and the strongest bridge across the Don at Kalakh. The German troops fighting at Stalingrad were now cut off from their supply base. Coming across the Volga and from the Kalmyk steppe, the Russian southern vanguard overcame the defences of the Romanian Fourth Army positioned there, blocked the railway coming from the south-west (Salsk) and, after a hard fight against the weak and hastily built-up German lines of defence, was able to reach the Don south of Kalakh where they were able to shake hands with the Russian troops arriving from the north.

Despite their immediate counterattack, the XLVIII Panzer Corps held in reserve on the Chir river was unable to prevent the encirclement of the Sixth Army (the larger portion of the Fourth Panzer Army was also trapped with them). This panzer corps consisted only of the 22nd Panzer Division, which was not at its best in terms of materiel, and the Romanian 1st Tank Division, which had recently been created and was not yet experienced in combat. Later, with help from the quickly created Army Detachment Hollidt, a new line of defence on the Chir river was built and strengthened with great effort.[viii]

---

viii Army Detachment Hollidt is also known as Group Hollidt in some contexts.

During the first days of the operation south of the Don, the Russians pushed slowly toward the south-west in the direction of Kotelnikovo, even though any great victories would have been denied them there – in the entire region between Elista and the Don, all that was left was the staff of the Fourth Panzer Army and two Romanian cavalry divisions with a total strength of 1,200 riders. The Russians had made their thrust between the staff of Fourth Panzer Army and its two divisions. The German security forces that were immediately formed from such elements as rear echelon staffs, supply troops, workshops, and so forth (Pannwitz, Mikosch, etc.), did in fact fight bravely, but were unable to withstand the strong enemy charge. This created a gap of 150km. The Russians did not seize this opportunity, possibly because they placed higher priority on the Stalingrad ring. More than that, they would face 19 German and two Romanian divisions, whose total strength of 200,000 men would stretch their capabilities.

To achieve a tighter consolidation of the participating armies on the German side, Army Group Don was created under command of Feldmarschall von Manstein. Under this command were placed the Sixth Army, the Fourth Panzer Army, and the Romanian Third Army. The remainder of the Romanian Fourth Army was assigned to the Fourth Panzer Army. Their stated mission was to bring the enemy attacks to a halt and win back the positions taken by the Russians.[1]

Army Group Don now received new forces: from Army Group B came Army Detachment Hollidt; from Army Group A came the general headquarters of LVII Panzer Corps, along with the battle-weary 23rd Panzer Division. Further additions included the 6th Panzer Division, which was still in the process of transport, and later, coming from further away, the 11th and 17th Panzer Divisions with some Luftwaffe (air force) field divisions, although these were not battle ready in terms of training and equipment.

Army Detachment Hollidt consisted of the 62nd, 294th, and 336th Infantry Divisions, and the XLVIII Panzer Corps. The XLVIII Panzer Corps included the 11th and 22nd Panzer Division, as well as the 7th and 8th Luftwaffe Field Divisions. These were tasked with halting the advance of the Russians at Chir, at the large bend of the Don river.

Afterwards, in concert with the Fourth Panzer Army, which had been reinforced south of the Don, they were to push on from the bridgehead at the mouth of the Chir to relieve Stalingrad.

The Fourth Panzer Army received the Corps Headquarters of LVII Panzer Corps, which was just arriving from the Caucasus, along with the 23rd Panzer Division. Later, LVII Corps Headquarters received the 6th Panzer Division, then later the 17th Panzer Division. The 17th Panzer Division had first been intended as a replacement for the 15th Luftwaffe Field Division, which never did appear. In addition to these larger German units, the Fourth Panzer Army also commanded the newly formed Romanian Army, with its VI and VII Corps. This Romanian army, however, in terms of equipment and fighting spirit, looked better on paper than in the field. The German 16th Infantry Division (motorised) at Elista, which was also under the command of the Fourth Panzer Army, could not be deployed; Army Group A inexplicably claimed that at that moment they were unable to free up any forces to replace them (after all, their very existence was at stake!).

The well proven 4th Air Fleet (Freiherr von Richthofen) was to provide support for the army group, with the additional task of ensuring supplies for the Sixth Army for the duration of their encirclement.

The reckless promise made by Göring to Hitler, of providing the supplies by air to Stalingrad, would prove catastrophic.

It was not the fault of the 4th Air Fleet that, due to a lack of cargo capacity, they were unable to fulfil this second task. From the very beginning they had maintained that this would be impossible. Yet through all the fighting, the dedication of their combat units and transport echelon exceeded all expectations.

At Kotelnikovo, the LVII Panzer Corps gathered for attack. At the large bend of the Don river the Russians increased their pressure, so that Army Detachment Hollidt could barely hold the mouth of the Chir. On 3 December, the day designated for the beginning of operations at Stalingrad, it was clear that no further help could be expected from that quarter.

CHAPTER II

The First Attack

3–4 December 1942
(Maps 3 and 4)

The terrain south of the Don
The enemy and his enemy assessment
The battle at Pokhlebin

The terrain around Kotelnikovo in early December 1942 was monotonous. In spring, the steppe may well have been a sea of flowers of rare beauty, but at that time of year there were only withered tufts of brown grass. Stands of trees were found only in the lowlands around the Don and near its tributary streams. Further to the south and east, hardly a bush was to be seen. The villages were scattered at long distances from each other; between them lay 10 to 20km of steppe, where only scattered collective farms could be seen. The terrain varied little, with its largest hills delineated by sections of streams. From this spot, in good weather, it was possible to see nearly 10km out with nothing to catch the eye. The village houses consisted of low mud-walled huts, whose rooms were half underground. Only at the edges of the villages were there signs of soil tillage. The primary livelihood was raising cattle.

This region presented an ideal terrain for a superior panzer unit, but with one major challenge – the deep drainage ravines. They could be 10 to 20 metres across and were often impassable. Because they changed year to year, even good maps were often of little help.

As it turned out, the winter of 1942 was not as brutal for us as the previous one because we were now further south (on the same latitude as Milan). In early December the steppe was blanketed by only a few scant centimetres of snow that melted in the warm rays of the sun during the day, and then froze during the cooler nights. In this weather, the ravines presented an obstacle, as they often stretched 10km or more and it was not always possible to drive around them. Driving up and down the slopes in snow and ice was also difficult, as neither studs on the panzers nor snow chains on the motor vehicles were of much help. Had we been able to lay a grid of some sort on the ground in the manner of a carpet, it might have helped. For the pioneers, who had to rely on whatever the environment could provide, the barren steppe offered little help (no wood).

The ice on the streams at this time of year was not yet hard enough to allow all of the vehicles in the division to cross without extra construction.

When Feldmarschall von Manstein and his staff arrived from the middle front (Witebsk) to assume command of the newly formed Army Group Don, the Feldmarschall took Generalmajor Raus, the division commander of 6th Panzer Division, with him in his personal train to Rostov. There, Manstein personally briefed Raus on the situation, and ordered him to unload his division in and south-west of Kotelnikovo (not Millerovo, as had previously been ordered). Raus was to place himself under the command of LVII Panzer Corps and halt the enemy advance there.

It was known that the Russians were pushing forward to Kotelnikovo at the southern bank of the Don on both sides of the railway lines coming from Stalingrad. They had one cavalry corps (the Russian IV Corps), which was reinforced with tanks, plus two infantry divisions. It was presumed that behind those units lay the Russian 3rd Tank Army, which, after having secured the ring around Stalingrad, would now attack.

On the morning of 27 November 1942, the first transport of the 6th Panzer Division rolled into Kotelnikovo. The train had hardly come to a stop when the Russians began an artillery attack and pushed their way into the city, and within a few minutes, our division suffered its first dead and wounded. The train station swarmed with enemy soldiers who had got past the security troops on the town's outskirts. The grenadiers jumped from their train cars with lightning speed and threw themselves into the train station, challenging the Russians with loud shouting and their empty weapons. That same day, with the help of additional transports, the train station and city were cleared, and the enemy thrown out.

Was there ever a more definitive example of an initial engagement in uncertain circumstances?

Now came transport after transport, some of which unloaded along open stretches, which is difficult for a motorised troop. Additional forces arrived from the division (parts of which unloaded north of the Don in Morosovskaya and came via Zymlianskaya to the assembly area by land march), and with their help, by the end of November a blocking position was constructed around the city as far as the Don. After their first attack the Russians did not further disrupt our unloading.

The 23rd Panzer Division was assigned its assembly area to the right of the 6th Panzer Division, but it was held up during its overland march from the Caucasus due to terrain difficulties (sudden temperature increases caused periods of mud). Except for its anti-aircraft and anti-tank guns, which had pulled ahead quickly, only a few of its units had arrived. The division had only just over 30 panzers. Its grenadier regiments, however, were fully filled.

The planned deadline for the attack, 3 December 1942, now proved to have been set too early. As yet, not even one element from the Luftwaffe Field Division had shown up. Whether the 17th Panzer Division would still arrive in time as a replacement remained undetermined. Even though the 17th Panzer Division was also reportedly much weaker in numbers, the exchange would be welcome. By then it had become apparent that the Luftwaffe field divisions were less able to cope with the harsh demands of the east, and it was better to have a neighbouring division that was proven in battle and could be relied on, regardless of its strength. When it came to the Romanian corps, not much could be said. They appeared to exist more in the planning than in reality. Their security forces, however, proved genuinely helpful in helping move panzers out of the repair shops (Pannwitz, Sauvant, etc.).[1]

The enemy was not expected to remain quiet any longer, and it was apparent that time and opportunity to head off a catastrophe were slipping away. On 2 December the first transports of 11th Panzer Regiment arrived and were greeted with relief. From the area of Remontnaya, where they were unloaded, the most recently arrived companies were thrown from the unloading ramp right into the heated battle.

The primary data sources for the beginning of all combat action in this area are the War Diary of the 11th Panzer Regiment, and later, from Battle Group Hünersdorff. The beginning of the fighting is documented in the following excerpts:

War Diary of 11th Panzer Regiment

Remontnaya, 3 December 1942

Second Company being unloaded and moving into cantonment area west of Remontnaya.

1015hrs.[2]

Call from Ia (operations officer) of the division: enemy attacking with tanks at Pokhlebin from the north. Division has moved 5th and 1st Companies to Kotelnikovo. Regiment must ready themselves for battle. Division orders: all companies forward. Regimental commander to division staff. Under command of II Battalion [Major Dr. Bäke[3]] will be 1st, 5th, 8th and 2nd Companies.[4] Staff of II Battalion, 8th, and 2nd Companies begin march toward Semichni. Battalion Bäke to be placed directly under the division.

1100hrs.

Enemy has broken through with tanks at Pokhlebin from the north, toward the south, and has overrun the 3/114th Panzer Grenadier Regiment which had been securing Pokhlebin.

1300hrs.

Seventh and 6th Companies unload in Gachun, south of Remontnaya. Commander [Major Löwe] and parts of Staff Company/I Battalion also arrive in the meantime.[5] Companies to move as far east as possible in cantonment area of the regiment, so that they can be quickly sent forward.

Enemy tanks south of Pokhlebin turned off west toward Mayorovski and were fought off by tank destroyers. Division had ordered 1st and 5th Companies and II/114th Panzer Grenadier Regiment (on SPWs) to attack this enemy.

What had happened? These enemy tanks were probably elements of the reinforced Russian IV Cavalry Corps, which had penetrated the division's security lines at Pokhlebin, and were attempting to go around Kotelnikovo. The first two companies of 11th Panzer Regiment (1st and 5th), unloaded on 2 December, were immediately moved forward, followed by companies and staffs, as they became available. Organising of the units prior to deployment was no longer possible; as a result, the company commanded by this author (6th Company), among others, was not with its own battalion (II), but instead went into battle with I Battalion.

If we could not stop this enemy soon, not only would the entire assembly of forces would be in jeopardy, but also the venture that was planned for later.

For a closer look into the enemy's intentions, the following attack orders for the Russian IV Cavalry Corps, which were captured in later fighting, are reproduced here in translation.

Captured Russian Orders

Verkhne Yablochni, 2 Dec 42 21.40hrs.[6]

Map 200 000[7]

Enemy continues its defence of Kotelnikovo with two infantry regiments and 40 to 50 panzers. The western perimeter of Kotelnikovo has been fortified by bunkers, especially in the area of the depot and M.T.S.[i] The area of Semichni has been built up as a fortified strongpoint. In the area of Zygan-Sacharovo, trench systems.

The IV Cavalry Corps (without the 61st Cavalry Division) is to occupy Kotelnikovo as of end of 3 December 1942 and will advance with one of the regiments into the area of Moloratiwrni [?] [brackets in original]. The 302nd Infantry Division is to push in general direction of the railway line toward Kotelnikovo and occupy the outskirts of Kotelnikovo.

---

i   M.T.S. = unknown abbreviation.

Link up with division only at Hill 142 (east of Chielnikovo), road fork 8km north-west of Grenyachi railway station Kotelnikovo.[ii]

On 3 December 42, by 1100hrs. the IV Cavalry Corps, in the first wave with 85th Tank Brigade, is to occupy Mayorovski, Sacharovo, Pokhlebin, and pushing from the west, take the western border of Kotelnikovo, then pursue the retreating enemy along the railway line to Dubovskaya [?].

The advance party (1st Company tanks, 1st Company motorised infantry) is to clear enemy out of Kudinovo, Hill 104.5; at 0900hrs. at Mayorovski, left of Kurmayarski Aksai river, advance party is then to move on the line from the fork in road at Kotelnikovo-Pokhlebin-Mayorovski and secure the exits of the 85th Tank Brigade and the 81st Cavalry Division in the area of Mayorowski-Pokhlebin. The starting point Vesyoli is to be passed though at 600hrs.

The 85th Tank Brigade is to enter the area of Mayorovski on 3 December at 1030hrs. and assemble in the ravine north-east of Mayorovski, run reconnaissance on Nagavskaya and place combat outposts in Potemkinskaya and Romathgliwki [?]. At 1300hrs. on 3 December, the brigade is to attack Semichni simultaneously with the motorised battalion (without 1st Rifle Company) and one cavalry regiment from 81st Cavalry Division. After the occupation of Semichni, the motorised battalion of the brigade is to be brought in for the occupation of Kotelnikovo. Main force is to pass through the starting point of Vesyoli at 0700hrs. on 3 December.

The 81st Cavalry Division with two batteries of the 149th Panzerjäger (anti-tank) Regiment are to assemble in area of Pokhlebin and the ravine south of there, leaving combat outposts in the strength of one platoon in Verkhne-Kurmoryaski. The mission is to attack and occupy the western border of Kotelnikovo together with two regiments, and with the 85th Tank Brigade. Beginning point for the attack is the road fork 3km east of Hill 60, single houses north-west of Hill 60. Attack will begin on separate order. Starting point of Vesyoli is to be passed through at 0730hrs.

First Cavalry Regiment with motorised battalion of the 85th Tank Brigade (without 1st Rifle Company) is to gather on 3 December at 1130hrs. south of the road fork Kotelnikovo-Pokhlebin-Mayorovski, with the mission of capturing Semichni. Start of the attack: 1300hrs. They are to be supported by 1st Tank Company. Leader of the group is Major Schavovarov, acting division commander of 81st Cavalry Division.

The 149th Guards Mortar Battalion (*GDM* = *Garde-Minenwerfer Battalion*) is reserve. Must be ready with manpower and firepower to hold down the defence

---

ii   All parentheses in original.

system in the area of Semichni and on the western border of Kotelnikovo. It is to move behind the 81st Cavalry Division.

The Training Battalion (without 1st Squadron), 4 [th?] Anti-Tank Battalion, two batteries from 149th Anti-Tank Regiment as reserve. Leader Captain Genyev will follow behind 81st Cavalry Division and assemble on 3 December at 1100hrs. in area of Hill 76 west of Vesyoli.

Two squadrons of the training section with two anti-tank companies are to hold section Verkhne Yablochni, in order to prevent any attempt by the enemy to break through toward the north.

At 1100hrs. the staff of IV Cavalry Corps is to be at Point 76 (south-east of Vesyoli), then Mayorovski, Semichni, and south-west edge of Kotelnikovo.

Report in: on arrival, on reaching the assembly area (Mayorovski-Pokhlebin), on readiness of the sections, on the beginning of the attack, and on the occupation of Kotelnikovo.

Signed:
Commander of the IV Cavalry Corps
Generalleutnant Meschkin

Commander of the Staff
Oberstleutnant Shvevtschuk

A close reading of this order can provide valuable insights, both in terms of form and content. In contrast to the German custom, for instance, the order goes into too much detail for corps level orders and gives too little emphasis on the end goal. For this attack the Russian corps had only the 81st Cavalry Division and the 85th Tank Brigade at their disposal (and according to paragraph two, the 61st Cavalry Division appears to be deployed elsewhere). Russian units were only slightly more than half as strong as the German units of the same designation, which meant that for this operation the Russian IV Cavalry Corps must have been approximately the size of just one German division.

Another surprising detail is that the assembly areas are situated in the middle of enemy territory (from the Russians' perspective). They considered an advance party (vanguard) of only two (!) companies strong enough to clear this area. Reflecting on the assessment of the enemy in

Paragraph One – incidentally a rather accurate image of their German enemy – this appears somewhat unreasonable, even when considering that the advancing Russian 302nd Infantry Division would be able to pin down a large number of the enemy (the Germans).

But to return to the course of events:

War Diary of 11th Panzer Regiment

1600hrs.

Call from Ia, enemy appears to have turned off. It is suspected that on the 4th the enemy will try to surround Pokhlebin from Kotelnikovo. Orders from the division:

Staff of Battalion I, with 6th and 7th Companies, to move to Korolev, west north-west of Semichnaya.

Regimental Staff to Division.

It is expected that after presenting the reconnaissance results to the division commander on 4 December, the commander of the panzer regiment will take over both sections.

1900hrs.

Commander is with battle staff at division.

First and 5th Companies advance on enemy tanks south of Pokhlebin at nightfall. The enemy, positioned behind a berm, allow the two companies to advance. One enemy tank destroyed, one of ours set afire (one dead, one wounded). Battle ends at nightfall.

Sixth and 7th Companies nearly veered off at Semichni during the night. The advance extremely hindered by the slippery ground. The ground is thawing, and the roads are muddy. The regimental commander and commander of Section I are ordered there on the early morning of 4 December. Depending on results of reconnaissance, the division commander will possibly order the regiment to attack under command of the regimental commander.

Initially, Battalion Bäke is to be placed under the command of the 114th Panzer Grenadier Regiment in Mayorovski; the enemy must be defeated at Pokhlebin. Third Company will be unloaded in Remontnaya and remain there on orders from the division. Fourth Company is to be moved forward to Semichni (on the transport train) and unloaded, with orders to remain there initially.

During these events, the Russian 302nd Infantry Division came under artillery fire on both sides of the railway line, which was coming from the north-east toward Kotelnikovo. It came to a standstill in front of the German Fourth Panzer Army, which was securing that area. Meanwhile, the Russian IV Cavalry Corps, which was advancing from the north toward Pokhlebin, having deployed a stronger tank force, overran 3/114th Panzer Grenadier Regiment.

Third Company deserves special praise for its lonely, devoted struggle there, as is shown in the following report from Oberst H. Zollenkopf, the then-commander of the 114th Panzer Grenadier Regiment:

Report
by
Oberst H. Zollenkopf

The 114th Panzer Grenadier Regiment (minus II Battalion SPWs), reinforced by an anti-aircraft battery (8.8 and 2cm), and relying on cooperation from elements of the 76th Artillery Regiment, was positioned in the area of Zygan-Pokhlebin-Mayorovski since early December, with the mission of securing this area.

In this security sector, the Kurmoyarski Aksai flows from the north. This stream, with its small tributaries, was something of a panzer barrier. The slightly hilly terrain with its thin layer of snow was passable for all motor vehicles as far as the Don. The security in Chudinov on the Don was so weak that it had little combat power for a defence; an enemy tank attack from the north on Pokhlebin and Mayorovski had to be expected.

Based on this situation assessment, the anti-tank *Schwerpunkt* (main effort) was to be at those two villages. The forces in all three villages were allocated as follows:

Mayorovski: 2/114th plus elements of 1/114th, one platoon of 8.8 anti-aircraft guns, one platoon from 9/114th (heavy infantry howitzer).

Staff: 114th Regimental and I/114th.

Pokhlebin: 3/114th, reinforced by one anti-tank platoon 5cm (motorised), one I Battalion infantry howitzer platoon, and forward observer

Zygan: This area is armour proof (*panzersicher*), needing only remaining elements of 1st/114th.

For the conduct of the battle, the division had ordered that the area of Zygan-Pokhlebin-Mayorovski must be defended. In the case of strong enemy attack, Group Zollenkopf itself would be surrounded. In this event, the intent was to lead the attack with the armoured groups (11th Panzer Regiment and II/114th Panzer Grenadier Regiment (SPW)), which were gathered further to the rear.

On 3 Dec 1942, at about 0830hrs., Leutnant Graf Plettenberg, commander of 3/114th Panzer Grenadier Regiment, arrived in Mayorovski to issue orders. He reported a quiet night.

At that moment, sounds of battle could be heard from the direction of Pokhlebin. Graf Plettenberg immediately rushed to his company and wired that some mounted enemy reconnaissance troops had attempted to engage but had been successfully fended off.

Other messages prior to 1030hrs. reported that the enemy had attacked with tanks, first with four, then with 12, but after having lost two, broke off the attacks. Then followed a report of 20 tanks (T34s), accompanied by enemy infantry, which after hard fighting, managed to break through into the northern part of Pokhlebin. The losses were not yet all known but were considerable. The Plettenberg company still held the southern part of the village and the terrain around the stream in the direction of Zygan. Then the wire connection broke off.

What had happened in Pokhlebin?

Near 0830hrs. several strong mounted reconnaissance troops from northern Pokhlebin approached. The Heavy Machine Gun Platoon Burian allowed them to get closer, and then destroyed the majority of them. The commander, Lt. Graf Plettenberg, ordered Oberfeldwebel Weidler and Feldwebel Riedel's platoons to perform reconnaissance, and he himself took command of one reconnaissance troop. After advancing about one hundred metres, they could see into a ravine that ran to the north and diagonally to the village. Here, several T34s with riflemen mounted on them and lorries carrying infantrymen were gathering for a thrust on Pokhlebin. The reconnaissance troops rushed back immediately, and the platoons took their prepared positions at the outskirts of the village. The German anti-tank soldiers positioned between the Weidler and the Riedel platoons waited for the enemy tanks to approach and fired on two of them. The enemy tanks turned back and disappeared into the ravine. Shortly afterwards the Russians attacked the village outskirts with trench mortars. Amid all of this, a large group of T34s with riflemen mounted on them attacked again, overran the anti-tank guns, and broke through into the village.

The platoons of 3rd Company/114th, however, allowed themselves to be passed up. Using both light and heavy machine gun fire, they attacked the enemy lorries filled with infantrymen, inflicted heavy casualties on the Russians, and forced them to back off while still outside the village. While the tanks, now separated from their infantry, penetrated further into the village, some hard, close-quarters fighting started on the outskirts of the village. The fighting was so fierce that platoon leader Burian, having shot his machine pistol dry, went after the Russians with a club. This battle against the tanks' accompanying infantry effectively broke the momentum of the tank attack and stalled its breakthrough, winning time for countermeasures to be taken. Casualties included the dashing young Leutnant Graf Plettenberg, who was killed in the midst of his troops, as well as the commander of Leutnant Möller's 1st Infantry Gun Platoon. All of the platoon leaders, Leutnant Tarner, Oberfeldwebel Weidler, and Feldwebel Riedel, were wounded. Altogether, two thirds of the defenders of Pokhlebin were out of the fight due to injury or death. The rest clung to the snowy slopes of the Kurmoyarski Aksai and attempted to make contact with 1/114th, which was performing security.

At around 1100hrs., the commander of I/114th, Major Hauschild, sent a liaison reconnaissance troop from Mayorovski to Pokhlebin. After a short time, it reported from an area south of Pokhlebin that enemy tanks were on the move in the area, and in the valley to the west were two battalions of infantry and several tanks conducting pre-combat checks. An enemy reconnaissance troop was moving in the direction of Mayorovski.

To avoid losing time in sending out a forward observer, the commander of the 114th, along with the NCO of the reconnaissance troops, attempted to bombard this gathering with artillery fire. The commander of the I/76th Artillery Regiment, Major Schulz, was already at the command post and ordered the NCO to observe some ranging shots with high angle airbursts. This manoeuvre was successful. With concentrated fire from the I/76th and one heavy battery, and with effective fire from the heavy infantry guns of 9/114th, the enemy's preparations for attack on Mayorovski were completely shattered.

At about 1230hrs., further reconnaissance reports from the Pokhlebin area indicated tank and infantry movements there. It was not clear whether the Russians intended to advance further towards Mayorovski or Kotelnikovo.

When the commander of the 114th Panzer Grenadier Regiment requested panzers and anti-tank guns, the division authorised two immediately available panzer companies for Pokhlebin, with a later addition of one anti-tank company.

Until about 1300hrs., a firefight was observed between several of our panzers and enemy T34s to the south of Pokhlebin. The German panzers apparently could not move forward because of a ravine. Tanks from both sides were on fire.

This unexpected resistance from the Germans (see the Russian orders, Paragraph 3, expressing opposite expectations), forced the Russians to prematurely pull stronger forces forward. The 6th Panzer Division, by bringing in reinforcements, was able to intercept the dangerous enemy attack south of Pokhlebin in good time. The Russians had pushed forward, and on the following day, the German commanders surrounded them with their newly, quickly acquired, armoured forces. Planned reconnaissance had to explore the basis for a coming attack.

War Diary of 11th Panzer Regiment

Semichnaya, 4 December 1942

The commander, along with battle staff and regimental staff, remains with the division in Semichnaya on the night of the 3rd and 4th. This is in order to be on hand on 4 December with two sections (six companies) for an attack, should the Luftwaffe reconnaissance determine strong enemy presence at Pokhlebin.

0245hrs.

Adjutant ordered to Ia. Reconnaissance reports sounds of tanks in Pokhlebin during the night. Division suspects enemy has received reinforcements – especially tanks – and orders an attack by the entire regiment as early as possible.

Units available for the attack:

Battalion Bäke with Staff of II Battalion, 1st, 2nd, 5th and 8th Companies

Battalion Löwe with Staff of I Battalion, 4th, 6th, and 7th Companies

II/114th Panzer Grenadier Regiment (SPW Battalion)

1st/41st Panzerjäger Battalion (with self-propelled gun carriage)

I/76th Panzer Artillery Regiment (one light and one heavy battery)

Fourth Company was ordered directly to Semichni upon unloading at Semichnaya, but had problems during unloading and did not arrive at Semichni until 0645hrs.

0530hrs.

Commander quickly briefs the section commanders in Semichni and then goes to commander of 114th Panzer Grenadier Regiment for briefing on the deployment with reconnaissance reports at hand.

Because reconnaissance was scheduled poorly and carried out late by the grenadier regiment, unnecessary time is spent waiting.

The reconnaissance results say nothing about the enemy tanks. Only in the ravine between Pokhlebin and Mayorovski have forward observers determined that enemy infantry has crept in.

Commander decides on an immediate attack on Pokhlebin from the west and north-west and sets the time for issuing of the order for 0830hrs., at the command post of the 114th Panzer Grenadier Regiment. The section commanders are instructed to bring their companies to the assembly area.

0830hrs.

Orders issued:

Attack Pokhlebin from the west and north-west. Destroy the enemy, capture Pokhlebin. Attack to be carried out as far as the Aksai river north of Pokhlebin.[8] Clear enemy from territory north and around Pokhlebin.

Right flank: 1/11th Panzer Regiment and 1/41st Panzerjäger Battalion (anti-tank battalion) is to hold back and prevent the enemy from retreating toward the south. The bulk of II/11th Panzer Regiment is to attack Pokhlebin, with the right flank at Mayorovski and with the *Schwerpunkt* to the left via Hill 76.6.

I/11th Panzer Regiment is to attack from Hill 94.4 with its *Schwerpunkt* to the left via Koslovaya ravine (2km north of Pokhlebin), from the north-west. II/114th Panzer Grenadier Regiment will follow between the two battalions in order to be quickly brought forward to the Pokhlebin-Vesseli road in case the enemy retreats to the north.

I/76th Artillery Regiment with two batteries will support the attack and take Pokhlebin and the nearby hills under fire before and at the start of the attack, in order to set the enemy in motion, creating targets for the panzers. Heavy anti-aircraft guns from Kotelnikovo will fire on Pokhlebin when notified by radio signal that the regiment has moved into attack position.

0945hrs.

I/11th Panzer Regiment reports all in ready position. Commander issues order to begin assembling.

The plan of attack was to surround the Russians from the left, as our panzers would be blocked by the Aksai river. This section of the stream would likewise block the enemy's retreat, as well, but the Russians didn't see this problem until the attack was underway. When they did catch on and began to move back, they met up with I/11th Panzer Regiment as it advanced toward Pokhlebin. This error in intelligence would cost them dearly.

War Diary of 11th Panzer Regiment

0955hrs.

The attack begins, but II Battalion only gains ground very slowly. The battalion attacks the hills of Pokhlebin frontally, and is met by strong, well-placed fire from excellently camouflaged enemy tanks and enemy anti-tank units. In a short time three tanks from the centrally positioned 8th Company take full hits and are out of action. The panzers explode. Several panzers from 2nd Company also burning from hits taken to the fuel cans attached to rear of the vehicle. The commander of 2nd Company abandons his burning panzer (from fuel canister fire) and is badly wounded once outside of the panzer. With the wounding of its commander, the company suffers loss in combat power.

Due to difficulties in orientation, I/11th Panzer Regiment, which was supposed to attack Pokhlebin from Hill 94.4 from the north-west, is too far to the north. In addition, the enemy force, which they want to intercept, has already moved even further north.

The regimental commander radios orders to I/11th Panzer Regiment to turn back around toward Pokhlebin, and then he drives from the combat zone to meet the battalion and brings it back from the north to Pokhlebin to deploy and support the unavoidably detained II/11th Panzer Regiment

With the help from I/11th, II/11th Panzer Regiment recovers strength and their attack wins further ground. The hills and village of Pokhlebin are captured at 1200hrs., from the west and north. After the wide sweep by I/11th Panzer Regiment, a gap opens between the two panzer battalions, which the enemy cleverly exploits and breaks through. Even though parts of the two panzer battalions and the SPW battalion immediately turn back, this cannot prevent a part of the horse-mounted enemy from breaking in. But despite this, the attack is still a success.

So far, II/114th Panzer Grenadier Regiment had followed behind the battle and is now ordered to clear the enemy from the combat zone. The terrain, with its troughs and deeply cut out areas, works to the advantage of the enemy. Here he is able to dig-in in front of 'Fortress' Pokhlebin, allow the panzers to roll on by and then bring his defence back to life. Therefore, the panzers are shelled again and again from close range, primarily with anti-tank rifles

After the capture of Pokhlebin, the enemy is pushed together into the valley between Pokhlebin and Mayorovski with its infantry and parts of its dismounted cavalry. Here, just before nightfall, 5th Company and two SPW companies are still clearing the valley of scattered enemy forces who were still fighting.

Shortly before darkness the regiment gathers at the southern exit of Pokhlebin. The battlefield is completely quiet. The results of the battle: 10 enemy tanks destroyed, 14 guns captured, 1,200 prisoners of war accounted for. Eight hundred more reported later by the SPW battalion, which remains in Pokhlebin. The clean-up of the battlefield on the next day brings in a great number of enemy rocket launchers, machine guns, and other equipment, along with 800 horses.

The battle was won by the high-speed attack by the bulk of the regiment (about 90 panzers). Third Company and the light platoons from the regimental staff and the staff of II/11th Panzer Regiment had not been unloaded until the day of the battle; several panzers are side-lined due to mechanical problems stemming from the night-march to the assembly area and the swampy, muddy road conditions.

A particularly important share of the victory belongs to the II/11th Panzer Regiment and the spirited and devoted struggle of 2nd and 8th Companies. Deserving of special recognition is Oberstleutnant Ranziger, Commander of 8th Company, who was shot from his panzer three times, each time going on to mount another panzer.

Our losses: one mechanised armoured ambulance (variant of SPW) and one SPW, as well as one self-propelled 7.62cm anti-tank gun, 8 dead and 28 wounded.

Five total missing in action (including one on 2 Dec.), 12 out-of-service panzers (including five panzers mechanically side-lined before the battle).

Prisoners from the battlefield state they were with the 81st Cavalry Division and the 85th Tank Brigade. This corresponds to information on orders belonging to the Russian IV Cavalry Corps, which were captured during the battle.

The combat zone is ordered to be vacated in the following sequence: II/114th Panzer Grenadier Regiment, with two companies, Pokhlebin; 7/11th Panzer Regiment, I/11th Panzer Regiment, Mayorovski; II/11th Panzer Regiment, Semichni.

The sodden roads and collapsed bridges prevent the implementation of the above ordered sequence.

Report on Pokhlebin Battle
by
Commander, 6/11th Panzer Regiment

During the night of 3–4 December we drove in total darkness and on very muddy roads to our assembly area north-west to Pokhlebin, only now and again receiving guidance from motorcycle messengers. At breaking daylight, II Battalion was to attack the village from the south and south-west with artillery support. At the same time, it was our mission to capture Pokhlebin by sweeping northward. My company, along with 7th Company (Hauptmann Gericke) and 4th Company (Hauptmann Wils) belonged to I Battalion. Behind us gathered the II/114th Panzer Grenadier Regiment (SPW).

Our two light companies (6th and 7th) took over the lead next to one another in broad wedge formation. Fourth Company was tiered right behind my company (I moved forward to the right) in order to monitor our attack with their long range (7.5cm, long) guns. The attack deadline was delayed somewhat, so that we did not move out until about 1000hrs.

I heard the marching order through my headset, 'Goldregen, marsch!' Goldregen (Golden Rain) was the code name for my company. At that moment I warned my two front platoons so that they would not collide with 7th Company, which rolled forward on my left. Then, during the crossing of one final flat ridge, the whole panorama of the Aksai sector north of Pokhlebin came into view. From 1,500 metres away, I saw the road that led to Pokhlebin, completely clogged with Russian vehicles and convoys. Further to the left, the road led almost as far as the Aksai and further on, to a ridge, which was also teeming with enemy, and among them, I could make out tanks. Opposite me lay the hills on the eastern bank of the river, and over all of this hung a grey, endless sky. There was little time left for contemplation; we began the battle immediately, and the enemy responded with flashing lemon-yellow muzzle fire of anti-tank guns and tank rounds. One glance to the left provided a view of Pokhlebin, which lay under artillery fire. Its valley was filled with clouds of smoke and dust.

We could not remain standing still like this, as we offered too good a target for the enemy. On orders from the battalion commander, Major Löwe, both of us forward companies made for the road under the protective fire of 4th Company, which was positioned in the centre. Firing from all guns (or cannons), with no shortage of targets, we rolled at high speed right into the middle of the Russians, blowing up anything that tried to get in our way.

While Gericke (7th Company) followed the retreating enemy northward, my rear was left open. Because I was protected on my east side, I turned south toward Pokhlebin. On the opposite side of the Aksai, large numbers of Russian soldiers were streaming up the slopes on foot while under German artillery fire, pursued by bursts from our machine guns and high explosive fragmentation shells. Soon I saw a large protective trench about 1km away that ran diagonally from the road. It was probably left over from the summer offensive, as presumably the Russians could not have dug it during the night. Later it was learned that it had been expanded into a tank obstacle south of Koslovaya ravine. The Russians had constructed their defence there, and we were soon caught up in a duel with anti-tank guns. On the hills south of Pokhlebin, we could watch II Battalion's battle. Some of their tanks were on fire, sending up black smoke clouds; in the binoculars I saw scattered black spots moving around between them. These were our tank crews escaping from their burning tanks.

Without fire support from heavy weapons, it would be difficult for me to capture the trench that lay before me. There was only one road across it, and it was occupied by enemy anti-tank guns. I radioed for support, and shortly afterward I saw artillery fire hit the trench. I never knew whether the hits came from 4th Company in response to my request, or whether the batteries south of Pokhlebin had come to my aid on their own initiative. In any case I decided to attack. To our amazement, on both sides of the road stood deserted Russian vehicles, and horses without riders, and camels racing around everywhere, bobbing about with their wide, sweeping steps. I led my company into the trench at a quick tempo, constantly jumping in and out of fire cover, and managed – by some miracle – to capture it without casualties. I was the first to drive across. While crossing, I saw the destroyed anti-tank weapons and their fallen crews. One had to admit that this enemy, while facing a superior force, had truly sacrificed himself. I radioed back immediately, ordering the artillery fire to cease at my location, and since I had no desire to be mistaken for an enemy tank, I requested confirmation of my position. The radio message had just ended, and I readied my company for the entry into the village. Promptly, the artillery fire at my location stopped, just as if we were on the exercise field. It now focused on the village, the eastern slopes, and far to the north behind me, apparently targeting the Russians in front of Company Gerike (7th Company). Such was the perfection of our artillery!

The village, about 1km away, offered us only light resistance. I decided, somewhat out of pride, to be the first to enter with my company. It was apparent that our attack enabled II Battalion to catch its breath and move closer to the village. I pushed on into the village and met almost only enemy infantry. The artillery fire stopped, and soon all that was left was the crackling fires from the burning huts. I was very proud to have accomplished this all without losses.

Soon we were able to shake hands with II Battalion, which was rolling in from the south-west. They had had it harder than us. Several panzers, even the armoured ambulance, had been shot up, and Dr. Repnow, our excellent and tireless staff physician, was wounded.

The grenadiers were given the rest of the panzers for mopping up. They were still engaged in tough battles and were bringing in large numbers of prisoners from all around.

The following report by the commander, Major Dr. Bäke, dated just two days afterward, documents the attack by II Battalion:

Battle Report
on the attack of 4 Dec 1942

II/11th Panzer Regiment

In the Field, 6 December 1942

On 4 December 1942 at 1000hrs., II Battalion stood ready in the hills north-west of Mayorovski with orders to capture Pokhlebin, which had been taken by the Russians on the previous day, and to destroy the enemy's combat force there.

The battalion was arranged as follows: 5th Company, right forward; 8th Company, left forward; 2nd Company, left rear, tiered formation; battalion staff, behind 8th Company; I Battalion, angled to the left; with II/114th at its rear.

At 1000hrs., the battalion received orders from regiment to assemble quickly, as the Russians were withdrawing toward the north.

Advancing rapidly in the north-east direction, under artillery fire, the battalion reached the hills south of Pokhlebin at about 1045hrs.

During the crossing of the hills south-west of Pokhlebin, the battalion ran into vigorous fire from anti-tank guns from the western edge of the village. The 8th and 2nd Companies particularly, as they were positioned nearest the village, returned fire with intense force. In doing so, 8th and 2nd Companies put a number of anti-tank guns out of action. Eighth Company also destroyed five T34s that were retreating to the north.

Despite this, the Russians succeeded in putting four combat vehicles from 8th Company out of the fight with anti-tank fire. Three panzers from 2nd Company were also put out of commission and several others damaged. During this firefight, 5th Company pulled into position south of Pokhlebin and engaged enemy anti-tank guns, infantry, and cavalry. Fifth Company succeeded in destroying a large number of anti-tank weapons.

At around 1205hrs., the battalion received a radio message that Company Scheibert had arrived at 800m north of the village of Pokhlebin. On this, the battalion advanced further in the direction of Pokhlebin. The battalion was able to cross the southern edge of Pokhlebin, and was able to destroy strong enemy infantry forces there, who were defending themselves against our attack with anti-tank rifles (*Panzerbüchse*) and armour-piercing hand grenades. Fifth Company advanced further to the south-west with orders to destroy the enemy infantry that had dug-in and established his field positions there. Fifth Company brought in 352 prisoners of war.

At 1430hrs., the battalion gathered east of Pokhlebin, and on orders from the regiment, began the march back to Mayorovski and Semichni.

Seventh Company remained as security with Battalion Küper back in Pokhlebin.[9]

Losses: 8th Company, 4 Panzer IVs hit, three of them total losses; 2nd Company, three Panzers hit; 5th Company, one burst barrel; Staff Company's SPWs destroyed.

Loss of personnel: 8 dead and 24 wounded.

Signed Dr. Bäke

Wehrmacht Report
5 December 1942

(Excerpt)

Between the Volga and the Don, the Soviets also strike on 4 December in a powerful tank attack, but without success. Seventy-five enemy tanks were destroyed, 13 immobilised in the shooting. The enemy suffers high losses in personnel and weapons. A hard attack by our own panzer troops destroys enemy tanks and cavalry forces, capturing 2,000 prisoners and 14 cannons.

It had been an auspicious beginning. Not only did we recapture our former positions but inflicted high casualties on the enemy. While it is true that the German side brought superior panzer forces to the battle, the fact remains that there was far greater infantry strength on the Russian side, not to mention powerful anti-tank units.

Our success was due mainly to our enveloping attack. The German commanders proved themselves far superior to the Russians in the layout of the operation and the interplay of the individual weapons. Then again, according to statements from captured soldiers, the Russian corps have not seen much prior combat. At the start of the Russian attack operations at Stalingrad, they had been moved forward from their previous location and garrison near the Afghan border. In previous engagements, they faced almost exclusively Romanian forces. Thus, when facing the combat power of a new, well-practised German panzer division, it was understandable that they would make some seemingly incomprehensible blunders.

And certainly, the German side committed its own blunders. There were too few grenadier forces available for a complete encirclement, so that large parts of the enemy succeeded in breaking out. Moreover, II/114th Panzer Grenadier Regiment (contrary to the attack order – see the War Diary of 11th Panzer Regiment) was too dependent on the I/11th Panzer Regiment.

In the designated sector, there were major difficulties in the terrain, which to some extent hampered the SPWs. With such a short distance to the attack target, II Battalion ought to have waited out the fight and then later moved in to occupy the gap.

During the first pure panzer attack, II Battalion's participation was not urgently needed. There was a predictably large gap between the two panzer battalions north of the Koslovaya ravine, where the enemy seeped through and moved on westward. Second Battalion was too far away, so that the gap could not be closed quickly enough. Later, during the clearing and mopping up of Pokhlebin and its environs, II Battalion was very much needed and was of great help in wiping out the last pockets of resistance and bringing in prisoners. But this too shows that too few grenadier forces were made available for this attack.

To what extent the division might have been able to free up infantry forces for this operation is unknown to this author. Of course, it had to fend off the enemy (302nd Russian Infantry Division) as it pushed simultaneously from north and north-east to Kotelnikovo.

Despite this, there were significant victories. It was to be expected that in future, the Russians would be more careful. They might also have brought in reinforcements, which could have stopped our entire attack from the start.

One very painful loss to the combat power of the panzer regiment was that of the commander of 2nd Company, Hauptmann Hagemeister, who died of wounds in the field hospital. Another was the total destruction of three Panzer IVs, the only real match for the T34.

In the following days the many free-roaming horses and camels formed a pleasant diversion, especially for the older officers and NCOs who had spent their earlier years in the cavalry. It would take a sharp order from the division to bring this 'circus' to an end.

CHAPTER III

Preparations for the Advance on Stalingrad

5–11 December 1942
(Map 5)

Situation of 6th Panzer Division prior to 11 December 1942
The deployment of the 4th Panzer Army
The situation at Army Group Don (9 December 1942)

The time prior to 12 December, the deadline finally chosen for the attack, was filled with anxiety, which becomes quite apparent in the following excerpts from the War Diary of the 11th Panzer Regiment:

Semichnaya, 5 December 1942

… At 1300hrs. the commander speaks with the battalion commanders in Kotelnikovo and issues reconnaissance orders for 6 December, so in case the enemy attacks Kotelnikovo from the north or east, we will be able to carry out a envelopment at the enemy's flank.

Semichnaya, 6 December 1942

… Regimental staff from Semichnaya to Kotelnikovo. Commander with battle staff held back because of new enemy situation. Enemy at Darganov, 40km east of Kotelnikovo, advances from the north by way of that area (Romanian sector) and has put out feelers [vorfühlen] Kotelnikovo via Peperichni. It is assumed that the enemy will reposition his tank forces (IV and XIII Tank Corps with about 300 tanks) there and will sweep around for a thrust on Kotelnikovo, or west of Kotelnikovo.

It is feared that in this instance (*Fall Otto*) (Plan *Otto*), we must stop and defeat the enemy tanks south-west of Kotelnikovo. The commander points out that this tank movement would be the decisive battle in liberating the Stalingrad pocket, for which all tanks available to the corps must be deployed *en masse*. Only if this enemy tank corps is defeated will the road to Stalingrad open, and we will be able to break through and rescue our units trapped there ...

... All units are standing by, ready to move quickly into in the area of Semichnaya-Verkhne Vassilyevski; should the enemy break through from Dragonov, we would attack from Sovyetskaya, 32km south-east of Semichnaya.

Semichnaya, 7 Dec 1942

Reconnaissance reports that Budarka, south-west of Kotelnikovo, is once again clear of enemy. Enemy appears reluctant to enter Kotelnikovo from the south-west.

It is reported that our bridgehead at Chiriskaya on the Don has been seized by the enemy. Deliberations underway as to sending necessary support to our bridgehead at Chiriskaya (*Fall Dora*).

Semichnaya, 8 December 1942

Order to move 5th and 6th Companies to Kotelnikovo at dawn; 3rd Company is to remain for the moment in Semichnaya. All elements in Kotelnikovo must be ready to march when the order to that effect arrives (anticipated at 0800hrs.), so as to capture Gremyachi Verkhne Yablochni.

0845hrs.

March readiness suspended. Further orders expected. Third Company relocating to Kotelnikovo. Meanwhile, the entire regiment is assembled in Kotelnikovo. Orders for 3rd Company are revoked. Company is to remain in Semichnaya, as new reconnaissance reports enemy motorised forces in process of advancing from Aksai by way of Shutov 2 in the direction of Darganov-Peperichni.

1100hrs.

Commander is ordered to Ia. Under discussion is the deployment of *Fall Dora*, *Wilhelm*, and *Otto*. It is anticipated that *Fall Dora* will take place. It will begin on 9 December 1942 at 0430hrs. Under command of the 11th Panzer Regiment will be:

II/114th Panzer Grenadier Regiment (mechanised),
III/76th Artillery Regiment with 6th and 9th Batteries,

the 8th and 10th Anti-Aircraft Training Regiment (*Flak-Lehr-Regiment*), and 3rd Company/61st Anti-Aircraft Training Regiment A.

Mission:

Starting out from Kotelnikovo, capture Gremyachi-Verkhne Yablochni (from the north), Nikhne Yablochni (also from the north), and Verkhne Kurmoyarski (if possible). Then the regiment is to advance further in the general direction of Generalovski.

Third Company is to move immediately to Kotelnikovo, along with the commander of the tactical operations staff of 11th Panzer Regiment This means the entire regiment will then be in Kotelnikovo. The regimental commander will order the battalion and battalion commanders under his command to area garrison headquarters at Kotelnikovo at 1630hrs. Orders are to be issued there.

The deployment for *Fall Wilhelm* and *Fall Otto* will have about the same task organisation as Group Hünersdorff; in *Fall Wilhelm* the group is to advance along the railway toward the north-east. The mission is to destroy the ring around Stalingrad. In *Fall Otto*, the goal is to destroy enemy forces coming from Aksai via Peperichni, in the attempt to capture Kotelnikovo from the south-east.

1800hrs.

Fall Dora is becoming unlikely, as in the meantime, reconnaissance reports motorised convoys with tanks from Shabalin to Generalovski and Aksai to Shotov 2. The *Dora* attack would have come between these two enemy motorised units, and moreover, the situation at the bridgehead Chiriskaya has been cleared up in the meantime.

2130hrs.

Call from division, *Fall Dora* is suspended. Regiment is to inform all applicable subordinated units.

Kotelnikovo, 9 December 1942

Commander is ordered to Unrein's command post.[1] Enemy tank forces brought to Shabalin are on the way to Krasnoyarski on the Don (about 100 tanks). It can therefore be assumed that these will be added to the rest of the 85th Tank Brigade, which battled the regiment at Pokhlebin on 4 December. It can be suspected that the enemy will again try to attack Kotelnikovo by attempting to sweep toward the west and from the north and come in (via Pokhlebin or Mayorovski). The enemy has occupied Koslovaya ravine (the northern one) 5km north of Pokhlebin, and some tanks were sighted. In this case, the *Unternehmen Nordwind* (Operation *North Wind*) is planned. In addition, the 11th Panzer Regiment and II/114th Panzer Grenadier Regiment are assembled at Semichnaya so as to destroy the enemy when it attacks, probably in the area of Mayorovski ...

Remontnaya, 10 December 1942

0730hrs.

Regiment received orders to relocate to the area of Semichnaya-Verkhne Vassilyevski with attached II/114th Panzer Grenadier Regiment. Companies to march one at a time [*einzeln-*, individually]...

Semichnaya, 11 December 1942

During the night, frost; in the morning, minus 6 degrees, light snow cover.

At 0600hrs., the tanks were started up and tested. By 0630hrs. all engines had been started. Some of the panzers had been started twice in the night, but the ones that had not still fired right up.

1000hrs.

Commander called to conference with division commander, which lasts several hours. The order to deploy on 12 December is issued. For concept of operations see Division Order No.7.[2]

The regiment and the II/114th Panzer Grenadier Regiment will move to Kotelnikovo at midday.

Issuing of order by Oberst von Hünersdorff.

These excerpts from the War Diary of the 11th Panzer Regiment reflect not only the respective enemy movements, but also the uncertainty and the constant changes that arose from developments on the southern front. They also reveal the friction between Army Group Don and the OKW.[3]

The newly formed Army Group Don struggled to convince Hitler and Generaloberst Paulus, commander of the surrounded army, to either permit an escape from the pocket, or to produce a decision from Paulus to break out. Meanwhile, the Fourth Panzer Army made preparations for its mission, which was to protect the flank of the advancing LVII Panzer Corps. This army had to assemble its forces without delay, organise the Romanian Fourth Army under its command for defence, and marshal all the fighting spirit essential to such a mission.

The attack deadline was postponed to the 8th, and later to the 12th of December, partly because of the uncertainty of coordinating with the trapped Sixth Army. Further, the bulk of the 23rd Panzer Division still had not arrived, and the XLVIII Panzer Corps. at the mouth of the Chir had not yet completed its advance, having had to fend off strong Russian attacks before it could fully assemble its forces.

The OKH (Army High Command) had the 17th Panzer Division unloaded behind the Don front on the left flank of the army group. It was the third unit that was to have replaced the 17th Luftwaffe Field Division, and it was promptly marched off to the LVII Panzer Corps south of the Don. There, Italians were facing the threat of a major Russian attack. The attack actually took place somewhat later, but meantime there was a suspenseful wait for their last-minute appearance on the battlefield.

The 6th Panzer Division was fully ready to deploy in the area of Kotelnikovo by about 5 December. The largest part of its grenadier forces and artillery served as security, and were positioned in a sweeping curved pattern from the Don, in front of Kotelnikovo, to about 15km east of the city. From here, they provided cover for the entire assembly area. The armoured group of the division was positioned around Semichnaya, which was further to the rear, so as to either intercept a direct enemy attack or encirclement.

On 11 December the decision was made. A decision *had* to be made, as further postponement would threaten the overall situation of the southern front; ultimately the rescue attempt would have to be suspended.

Fall Otto was abandoned.[4] The 23rd Panzer Division was now fully deployed, and the enemy moved hesitantly near the deep right flank and was no longer considered a threat. This operation, like *Nordwind,* was planned for use only if the enemy were to attempt to seize the initiative by attacking. The main goal had not been to attack and destroy the enemy in this area, but rather to break open a supply corridor to the Stalingrad pocket.

Fall Dora had a certain appeal.[5] This plan was to reach the objective in two leaps across the bridgehead of the XLVIII Panzer Corps at Chiriskaya. *Dora* was also abandoned, however, as the bridgehead was barely holding on. This front was pushed back by the Russians on 14 December.

Thus, what remained was to make a frontal attack on both sides of the rail line Kotelnikovo-Stalingrad. This was also the shortest route. Naturally this attack would draw in all enemy forces, and with this, not only resolve the uncertain situation on the right flank, but also bring relief to the XLVIII Panzer Corps, which was presently engaged in a hard fight. As was later learned, the Russians had left the southern part of their encirclement exposed in order to counter this threat.

Although there were likely reservations as to whether the two German panzer divisions alone could fight through the 150km from Kotelnikovo to the ring around Stalingrad, the matter could not wait any longer. There was still hope that the 17th Panzer Division could be brought in quickly enough for reinforcement, and that finally, in one last combined attack, they could reach the objective. Despite the previous failed attempts to do so, those in command positions at the southern front were certain they could still convince Generaloberst Paulus to break out of the encirclement.

The Fourth Panzer Army was engaged in a struggle to relieve the Sixth Army's situation, but the Sixth Army provided no help of any kind. The last possible chance to relieve Stalingrad, although a weak one, was the last-minute deployment of the 17th Panzer Division.

Considering the overall situation, an additional attack would be taking a risk on a scale not seen in the previous war, except perhaps once.

The following situation assessment dated 9 December 1942 was written by Generalfeldmarschall von Manstein as commander in chief of the army group, and sent to the Army High Command, describing the situation in the sector of Army Group Don.[6]

Letter from von Manstein

Top Secret
By Hand of Officer Only   9 Dec 1942

To: Chief of Staff, OKH

Operations Section OKH

Situation Assessment

1. Enemy assessment. In the last 10 days, the enemy has brought in strong forces for deployment against the army group. Most importantly, still more forces in addition to the reserves expected in the situation assessment of 28 Nov, number Ic. It has been determined that the total forces facing this army group are: 86 infantry divisions, 17 infantry brigades, 54 armour brigades, 14 motorised brigades, 11 cavalry divisions, totalling 182 large units. In addition, another 13 independent armoured regiments and single tank battalions and anti-tank brigades.

In specific:

a) The fortress area Stalingrad is encircled on the Volga front by the Russian 62nd Army with eight infantry divisions, three infantry brigades. One tank brigade in front, two infantry brigades, two tank brigades, two motorised brigades in reserve.

   On the northern front by the 66th and 24th Armies with total of 17 infantry divisions, one motorised brigade in front, four infantry brigades and four tank brigades in reserve.

   On the western front by the 65th and 21st Armies with total of 10 infantry divisions, seven tank brigades, two motorised brigades, five tank regiments, one anti-tank brigade in front, four tank brigades in reserve.

   On the southern front by the 57th and 64th Armies with total of seven infantry divisions, six infantry brigades, six tank brigades, six motorised brigades, two tank regiments in front, and apparently two infantry divisions, two infantry brigades, five tank brigades, one motorised brigade, and five tank regiments in reserve.

   In the last 10 days the enemy has attacked alternately between the north, west, and southern fronts. His main pressure no doubt lies on the western front. He is relatively weak on the south-western front.

b) Our advance on Stalingrad faces following enemy forces:

Toward the south-west, at the Chir front – the 5th Tank Army with 12 infantry divisions, five cavalry divisions, two motorised cavalry divisions, four tank brigades, one tank regiment, two motorised brigades in front, with two infantry divisions, four tank brigades, and one motorised brigade in reserve.[7] To the north, adjoining these and positioned in front of the centre and the left flank of Group Hollidt, are three more infantry divisions. Toward the south and east of the Don we face the 51st Army, with four infantry divisions, four cavalry divisions, one tank brigade, one motorised brigade in front, one tank brigade in front, and one infantry brigade in reserve. The gathering of more motorised forces behind the front is still not clear.

c) The recent days' reconnaissance reports: unloading eastwards of Stalingrad, as well as troop movements across the Don in front of the eastern front of Group Hollidt toward the south. Although the enemy's security front east of the Don is basically passive, apparently because the gathering of rear motorised forces has not yet been completed, the enemy did attack at the Chir bridgehead and west of Chir train station on the other side of the Chir with strong forces. As evidenced by the north-south movements in front of Group Hollidt, an expansion of this attack further westward is to be expected.

d) In the previous battles, the enemy no doubt sacrificed a considerable proportion of his tanks, but he compensated for the loss by bringing in new tank regiments. The attack strength of his infantry is still weak, but artillery activity on Stalingrad's west front has increased considerably.

2. Our Situation.

a) The Sixth Army has so far defeated all enemy attacks, although with considerable losses. Its present combat strength will be treated in a special report. The munitions supply in the essential types of munitions (shown in percentage of the initial supply effective 5 December 1942) totals:[8]

5cm towed cannon propelling charge/60 = 59.0%
7.5cm towed cannon propelling charge/40 = 39.4%
15cm mortar = 25.0%
Light Field Howitzer = 34.0%
8cm mortar = 30.8%
Heavy 10cm cannons/19 = 21.6%
Light Infantry Gun = 28.0%
Heavy Field Howitzer = 36.0%
Heavy Infantry Gun = 25.0%

The present supply of rations, after reduction to 200g bread, leaves enough bread until 14 Dec., midday rations until 20 Dec., evening meals until 19 Dec.

Despite excellent efforts by the Luftwaffe, the resupply by air only brought in 300 tons, due to weather conditions. Out of 188 aircraft used that day, two were shot down and nine lost. On all other days, the rations flown in totalled between 25 tons (27 Nov.) and 150 tons (8 Dec.) despite a minimum daily need of 400 tons.

b) The 4th Panzer Army. Due to bogging down of wheeled elements of 23rd Panzer Division, the assembly of the LXII Panzer Corps with its aviation combat squadrons will not be fully completed on 3 December as hoped, but on 10 December.

In order to salvage the situation at the Chir front, the XLVIII Panzer Corps (336th Infantry Division and 7th Luftwaffe Field Division) had to be deployed immediately. The battle is not yet over.

c) Romanian Units. At this time the Romanian Fourth Army is holding its position to the north, adjoining the 16th Infantry Division (motorised). But in the event of an attack of any strength from the north, it cannot be expected to hold. It has been all the more compromised due to instructions from Marschall Antonescu to avoid getting marooned.

d) The Romanian Third Army, except for the Romanian 1st Army Corps, which is assigned to Group Hollidt and is more or less intact, the battle strength of the remaining deployed Romanian divisions does not amount to more than one or two battalions. Artillery is not available in any degree worth mentioning. The restoration of units to the rear has not led to any significant results as yet due to lack of weapons. The fact remains that the Romanian commanders do not act with the necessary force. They characterise the defeat as having been 'caused by higher powers', meaning the German leaders. For the rest of it, the entire front manned by the Romanian Third Army is held by reaction forces, furlough units, etc. Without artillery and anti-tank guns, one cannot even make a show of strength. Long term, this front is not up to an attack from strong enemy forces, especially armoured forces. The cobbled together units, which lack a strong inner structure, must be replaced with combat units for the foreseeable future. Their composition and battle strength do not permit a long deployment on the front lines. Even when it comes to special troops withdrawn for rear duties, they cannot perform their individual duties long term without harm to the entire supply system.

3. *Our Intentions.* The army group intends, as soon as at all possible, to begin attacking with the Fourth Panzer Army, as reported, so as to establish communications with the Sixth Army. At this time, however, the thawing of the ground prohibits an advance by the LVII Panzer Corps.

Whether the divisions of the XLVIII Panzer Corps at the Chir front can be completely released on 11 December, is not yet certain. The participation of the 17th Panzer Division for this attack is necessary and has been ordered. Because it must be taken into account that the enemy could expand his attack on the Chir front in the general direction of Morosovskaya in the foreseeable future, the relief of this front must take place, either with the help of Group Hollidt with an attack in the general direction of Perelasovski, or by releasing a German division to us.

4. *Overall Assessment.* The mass of forces that the enemy has brought in to face the Army Group Don, leaves no doubt that he sees the *Schwerpunkt* of his overall operation here. He will continue to bring in more forces from other fronts as long as possible.

Therefore, no matter how the situation with respect to the Sixth Army may develop in the near future, a constant addition of forces to Army Group Don will continue to be necessary. It is crucial that all means be used to bring in the reinforcements more quickly. At present rate, we will have to remain at a disadvantage. I also consider it necessary that everything be done to make the Romanian armies functional, especially in terms of their willingness to fight, and to restore their trust in the German leaders.

As to the question of whether, after establishing communications with Sixth Army, we will be able to bring them out of the pocket, here are my own thoughts to consider:

a) If the Sixth Army were to be left in the fortress area, it is quite possible that the Russians, too, will hold out stoically and gradually bleed themselves out in pointless attacks, and that Stalingrad will become the final resting place for its attack power. But one must also be clearly aware that the Sixth Army has to live and fight under especially unfavourable conditions in the fortress area, and that with the present ratio of forces, which will continue for a long time throughout the area, the possibility exists that communications with them could break down again. In any case, a decisive change of situation in the coming weeks cannot yet be expected.

b) On the other hand, one must also take into account that the Russians might act properly [in terms of conventional doctrine], and while maintaining the pocket of Stalingrad, attack with strong forces in the area of the Romanian Third and Fourth Armies, with Rostov as their target. This will render our essential forces operationally static in the Stalingrad fortress area and tie us down trying to keep the communications open, while the Russian will have freedom of action across the entire rest of the front of the army group. To me, maintaining this situation over the entire winter appears pointless.

c) To pursue the decision, to keep Sixth Army in Stalingrad, must necessarily also be the decision to fight this battle through to a decisive victory. This depends on:

aa) Providing additional forces to Sixth Army for maintaining its defensive power, by sending in Luftwaffe field divisions to be incorporated into the army units.

bb) Above all, support of the connecting fronts of the Romanian Fourth and Third Armies with German forces, since holding of these fronts with the remnants of Romanian units and emergency fill-in troops is not assured long term.

cc) As soon as our forces permit, a serious offensive with the goal of definite victory.

The issue of whether the forces can be made available for this in a timely way lies outside my purview.

Commander in chief of the Army Group Don

signed,
von Manstein
Generalfeldmarschall

Ia No 0354/42 Secret, for Command Hqs.

CHAPTER IV

The Advance

12–24 December 1942
(Maps 6–15)

The breakthrough (12 December)
The capture of the Aksai Sector (13 December)
The battle for Verkhne Kumski (14–19 December)
The night march to the Myshkova (19–20 December)
The battle for Vassilyevka (21–24 December)
The end of the fighting (24 December)

War Diary of 11th Panzer Regiment[1]

12 December 1942

The readiness procedures are delayed, as the march across the bridge at the northern exit of Kotelnikovo is proceeding more slowly than expected. Further, the arrival time of 0430hrs. will not be possible, as it will still be dark.

0515hrs.

All units have reported in: 'Ready.'

0520hrs.

It has begun.

The attack proceeding as ordered. West of Hill 129, the panzer regiment is to move north, then turn off eastwards toward Gremyachi.

Order of battle: I/11th Panzer Regiment, II/11th Panzer Regiment

Hill 129 pinned down by artillery fire and ultimately cleared by II /114th Panzer Grenadier Regiment. Meanwhile, I/11th Panzer Regiment, after reaching the rail line to the east and north, secures area. Then II/11th Panzer Regiment swings in toward Gremyachi and after short battle captures it. Two panzers lost due to mines, one more destroyed by anti-tank system.

Meanwhile, I/11th Panzer Regiment is deployed northward along the rail line as far as Nebykovski station. In a valley to the south-west, a short battle ensues with one enemy 12.2cm battery and field positions, which ended at 0730hrs. Overall, enemy resistance is not hard. Two Stalin's organs [Katyusha, a mobile rocket launcher] open fire, which is unpleasant but causes little damage. In addition, enemy vanguards are engaged by our reconnaissance.

Those involved in the attack were surprised by the enemy's apparent lack of strength. Based on our own successful breakthrough, we were fully convinced of our own capability and were ready to face strong resistance. If not right away, then we expected it would appear further on at the narrow pass at the Nebykovski Station. This narrow passageway was also used by the railroad line to Stalingrad and was bordered by deep sand dunes so it could not be circumvented by motorised troops and could have provided an excellent barricade for the enemy's defence. It would be no exaggeration to call this a portal to the Aksai.[2]

How could the enemy's surprising absence be explained? We could not assume that he had simply made a mistake, or that he was not expecting an attack. Considering the Russians' forceful reconnaissance in the previous days, their experience in Pokhlebin, and their own country's well-functioning intelligence service, it ought to be obvious to them that the Germans had gathered their forces, and that their numerous panzers were not there simply for the sake of defence.

Then we came to our own realisation that, like us, the Russians did not have unlimited forces available. At that moment, they most likely considered the fortress around Stalingrad to be their main priority. Because of the enemy's conduct in front of the LVII Panzer Corps, we began to suspect that, not only had he sent his very best divisions to Stalingrad, but he had also withdrawn artillery and other heavy weapons from the Kotelnikovo front. He took this risk perhaps in the assumption that the Germans would not counterattack until later. Thus, it must have been a considerable surprise when the Germans appeared so soon. And we intended to take full advantage of the element of surprise.

Our first destination, the Aksai river, lay within close reach to both us and to the enemy, whom we believed to be at Verkhne Yablochni. In order to neutralise this flank threat, and to help Group Unrein (Battle Group from 4th Panzer Grenadier Regiment – without panzers), 6th Division decided to attack Verkhne Yablochni with Battle Group Hünersdorff (armour battle group consisting of: 11th Panzer Grenadier Regiment – II/114th Panzer Grenadier Regiment, among others), which had proceeded to this area from the south. At Nebykovski station, turning toward the north-west, the forces reached an area about 6km north-east of the targeted village at about 0830hrs., almost without enemy contact.

War Diary of 11th Panzer Regiment

0854hrs.

I/11th Panzer Regiment is positioned on Hill 124.7 with the regimental commander. The II/114th Panzer Grenadier Regiment is ordered to move to a position to the right of I/11th so as to secure the refuelling stop. The fuel and ammunition transports arrive surprisingly quickly. During this time, the II/11th Panzer Regiment also catches up and closes ranks. The artillery moves into position, and the anti-aircraft unit creates an air defence barrier toward the north.

For the attack operation in the direction of Stalingrad, the 6th Panzer Division had been organised into four battle groups, three of which were actually rather weak panzer grenadier groups (Zollenkopf, Unrein, and Quentin), plus the very strong Battle Group Hünersdorff. About four hours after the start of the attack, the following scene erupted.

While Zollenkopf (from the 114th Panzer Grenadier Regiment – minus II Battalion (SPW) among others) dominated the area north of Pokhlebin, to the left between the Don and Kotelnikovo, Unrein attacked almost due north towards Verkhne Yablochni. Hünersdorff was positioned to the north-east of this village, and Quentin (consisting mostly of the 6th Reconnaissance Battalion), initially following Hünersdorff, turned with its right flank on the railway line toward Stalingrad (the boundary of 23rd Panzer Division), and headed towards Chilekov.

It was known that the 23rd Panzer Division had also succeeded in capturing ground toward the north-east. This left a gap of about 30km in the Russian front. Resistance was detected only in Verkhne Yablochni and on both sides of the railway line. Unfortunately, at Chilekov there was another one of those narrow ravines that unexpectedly turned up in this region.

War Diary of 11th Panzer Regiment

1010hrs.

Arrival in Verkhne Yablochni. I/11th Panzer Regiment on the right, II/11th Panzer Regiment on the left, and between them, the panzerjägers on self-propelled guns. II/114th Panzer Grenadier Regiment follows in a broad wedge formation. The attack commences, initially according to plan and without enemy resistance, but then becomes stuck due to problems in the terrain. After withdrawing, the regiment deploys again toward the village, which it captures after a short fight against anti-tank and infantry weapons. Two enemy tanks manage to escape at first but are destroyed by anti-aircraft guns (*Flak*) at the panzer barricade at Hill 124.7. Second Battalion/114th Panzer Grenadier Regiment clears the area and finally hands it over to Group Unrein, which has arrived from the south according to plan. The regiment regroups and leaves for Chilekov by way of Hill 124.7 at 1330hrs. (1530hrs. local time), arriving at Chililov at nightfall. Chilekov has meanwhile been captured by Group Quentin. What made the entry to Chilekov difficult was an iced over ravine which was enough of an obstacle to prevent the last units from crossing until next morning at 0530hrs. (0730hrs. local time) During the night, I/11th Panzer Regiment shelters at the Chilekov Train Station, the II/11th Panzer Regiment overnights in the dairy 2km to the west north-west, while the II/114th Panzer Grenadier Regiment spends the night in the stockyard to the south-west. Little is available in terms of quarters, so almost everyone has to sleep in their vehicles.

Daily Report:

Captured goods: five tanks, 10 cannons, 10 anti-tank weapons, one Stalin's organ[i], a number of lorries, many small arms, 450 prisoners of war, five motor vehicles destroyed.

---

i   This is the name the German's gave to the Katyusha, a mobile rocket launcher.

The intent for the next day is to cross the Aksai at Klykov or Salivski and capture the hills north of there. Intent approved by the division.

Thus ended the first day of the mission to liberate the surrounded troops in Stalingrad. The important objective of the day, capturing the Aksai bridge, was not accomplished. In retrospect, one must doubt the wisdom of having decided to first capture Verkhne Yablochni, considering the few enemy forces found there. The village would have been captured in any case during the course of the day, probably by Group Unrein. In any case, Unrein's battle strength would have sufficed to tie down the Russians who were there, which would have averted a threat to the division's main forces advancing along the railway line. Nevertheless, as General Lee remarked after his unsuccessful battle at Gettysburg in 1863 to a member of his staff – in fact, this staff member happened to be the grandfather of this book's author: 'Captain, tomorrow every printer's apprentice will have some opinion about how I should have acted. It is only too bad that these strategists are so far away from the battlefield when they are needed.'[3]

As it turned out, we still had to face the frozen-over ravines at Chilekov, which, even with ice studs, were incredibly difficult.[4] Even though this became easier during the day with help from the pioneers, the cost in time was so high that any further advance had to end at nightfall, which set in very early at that time of year. Only later did we realise that it was possible to conduct very successful tank attacks – even actual raids – in this terrain, even at night.

The evening reports showed that the other groups had problems as well. The Russians might have sent only weak forces against our division, something we had not planned for. Or the Russians might also have withdrawn their main forces across the Aksai. We would find out the next day; hard fighting was expected.

During the night, no enemy was to be seen around Chilekov. Before us lay the same scene. Fires burning in almost all directions, quivering balls of light, and the repeated flickering of machine gun fire from the security forces. With no strict orders against it, they often shot at night, perhaps for the same reason dogs bark at night – to drive away uncertainty, or to just to demonstrate one's strength for its own sake.

It became bitterly cold, and the unit leaders didn't sleep. The ravine, its road no longer visible under the slippery, icy covering, required their constant focus. Then we also had to refuel, replenish ammunition, supervise the distribution of rations, attend meetings, and review orders for the next day.

No one was quite satisfied with how the day had gone. The question was, where were the Russians?

War Diary of 11th Panzer Regiment

0400hrs.

Issuing of orders by Oberst von Hünersdorff

0500hrs.

Fall-in at vehicle observation point north of Chilekov Train Station. The regimental commander [Hünersdorff] rejects the division's plan to deploy the panzers at night in order to capture the Aksai bridge. It is far too hard to keep one's bearings at night, and the frozen ravines present too great a risk for panzers. In accordance with orders, we are to fall-in at 0500hrs. and proceed to the sharp bend of the railway line, 2km west of the railcar siding area at Birykovski. The advance will be delayed further due to two frozen-over ravines. At this sharp bend, there is a short firefight with enemy tanks east of the railway. Group Quentin, advancing eastwards of the railway, requests support against these tanks. The commander has decided, however, not to allow ourselves to be pulled toward the east, but instead orders us to continue on north-west toward Salvaki.

Over the course of 12 December, the 23rd Panzer Division was not able to advance to the hills of Chilekov, as they still had unprotected flanks. In order to secure their flanks, Group Quentin, which was located alongside with the tanks on the opposite side of the rail line, had to move across the tracks. This enabled the 23rd Panzer Division to continue its advance. While Unrein and Zollenkopf followed on the left, in echelon formation, Battle Group Hünersdorff pushed on ahead. Taking the quickest route possible to Aksai permitted by the difficult terrain, they arrived at Chilekov, having had almost no enemy contact.

Despite calls for help, Hünersdorff refused to be diverted. Although he was in defiance of orders from division, he was able to avoid the mistakes from the previous day. With the first warm rays of daylight, the group reached its assigned sector. At that time, all that was known of the 23rd Panzer Division was that its desired objective for the day was also Aksai.

War Diary of 11th Panzer Regiment

0800hrs.

The bridge is taken with almost no enemy resistance. It is in bad shape but can be made ready for all vehicles. The I/11th Panzer Regiment moves across that sector to the north, and readies for an attack on Verkhne Kumski, which still had to be captured. After I Battalion crosses the bridge, the regimental commander follows, upon which the bridge fails. The commander's panzer sits blocking all further vehicles, and all attempts to tow it off prove unsuccessful. Once I Battalion crosses, no further forces can cross. The original plan was an attack by the entire regiment, with II Battalion/114th Panzer Grenadier Regiment, and the artillery. After a heavy Stuka attack on Verkhne Kumski, the commander decided to attack with only I Battalion/11th Panzer Regiment At 1200hrs., against weak enemy resistance, we took Verkhne Kumski.

Battle Group Hünersdorff had advanced over 25 kilometres within seven hours, had captured the Aksai bridge against weak enemy resistance, and had secured a 10 kilometre-deep bridgehead. It had left the bulk of the division, as well as its neighbouring unit to the right (23rd Panzer Division) far behind. It appeared that they would have an enemy-free route in the direction of Stalingrad.

But the question remained: 'Where are the Russians?' Their traces were everywhere, but never in any numbers worth mentioning. Their previous losses were not so great as to suggest that they had been totally destroyed. It had to be assumed that the Russian troops lay further to the rear, either in the region between Salivski and the Don, or to the right, in front of the 23rd Panzer Division, or possibly in both areas. But where was the mysterious Russian 3rd Tank Army? As to the threat of the German advance, the Russians couldn't possibly remain in a state of disbelief.

Thus, despite the peaceful silence, the situation did not allow for a relaxed attitude, especially considering that the Aksai bridge at Salivski was now impassable. A splintering of the division's main force had to be avoided. This meant that above all, the weak point at Salivski had to be reinforced, as this was where the remainder of the battle group would remain until it became possible to cross to the opposite side of the river.

Because Group Quentin remained tied down by the enemy, further to the right and rear, Unrein had to quickly reposition itself, while further to the left and rear, Zollenkopf and the Romanian VI Corps provided security. The I/11th Panzer Regiment, positioned far forward in Verkhne Kumski, was almost without supporting units, and to bring them reinforcements meant the bridge had to be repaired quickly.

War Diary of 11th Panzer Regiment

The following equipment is to be sent forward: one motorcycle rifle company, the two scout platoons of 11th PanzerRegiment, and two platoons from II /114th Panzer Regiment, mounted on panzers, which are still located on the opposite bank. Security for the bridgehead is to be taken over by I/4th Panzer Grenadier Regiment, with 1st Battery/76th Artillery Regiment.

Despite all efforts, the panzer lodged in the bridge cannot be removed. Therefore, Bridge Convoy K will be brought in and at 1200hrs. will begin with the bridge construction across the Aksai. On orders from division, II/11th Panzer Regiment was tasked with scouting the terrain south of the Aksai as far as the Chilekov ravine. No enemy tanks were found. Division also tasked 1st Company 41st Panzerjäger Battalion to do the same on Hill 56.3, which was 2km south of Salivski, since there 'ought to be' tanks there. Previous reconnaissance only revealed that the village Vodyanski was occupied by the enemy, and that at Dorofeyevski, 3km to the west, enemy cavalry has moved across a fording point toward the south. Since the bridge will not be completed until about 0500hrs, orders will be issued at 0400hrs. During the night, several surprise fire attacks by Stalin's organs at Salivski, in which even the regimental command post is hit and incurs some casualties.

The construction of the bridgehead and the capture of Verkhne Kumski took place against orders from the division, which had wanted the regiment to turn toward the tanks eastwards of the railway. Apparently, the enemy had systematically cleared out of the Aksai sector. Due to their quick action, the regiment prevents the formation of a strong centre of resistance at Verkhne Kumski.

The destruction of the bridge across the Aksai at Salivski brought an end to the advance on that day at 1200hrs. It was an ironic stroke of fate that the fault lay with commander of the battle group and his own panzer. Unfortunately, the panzer proved impossible to tow away, and its presence there prevented any restoration of the old bridge within the time available. A completely new bridge had to be constructed.

Then darkness brought everything to a halt, just as on the previous day. All that went on was reconnaissance, security, and the arrival of additional elements of the division.

The task given to II/11th Panzer Regiment, to search the terrain south of the Aksai in the direction of Chilekov ravine, was in response to a call for help by the rather weak 23rd Panzer Division, which had to fend off an attack by a strong Russian force shortly before reaching the Aksai and was unable to advance further. To deal with a possible threat from the east, the 6th Panzer Division commander decided to push in that direction with elements from two different units. This operation involved just two companies from II/11th Panzer Regiment and one SPW company from II/114th Panzer Grenadier Regiment. This drive was undertaken as a secondary effort, as the two other companies of the panzer battalion were needed to provide security toward the west, in the direction of Vodyanski. The author and his company participated in this advance.

Despite what is reported in the War Diary, it should be stated that we not only reached the Chilekov ravine but crossed it. Shortly before reaching the railway line, we came upon enemy tanks, but once we opened fire, they turned off northwards. As it later turned out, this enabled the 23rd Panzer Division to catch its breath and use the time to finish constructing two bridgeheads across the Aksai by nightfall on the same day.

All of this meant that any issues with the right flank of Battle Group Hünersdorff and its situation at Salivski had been overtaken by events: its earlier decision to avoid becoming diverted eastwards prior to the construction of a bridge at Aksai was validated. The main concern now was the area west of Salivski and the entire region around Verkhne Kumski. It was certain that a larger fight could be expected next day; the entire responsibility for reinforcing that far-forward point fell to the division and Battle Group Hünersdorff. Heightened reconnaissance activity would be crucial.

Wehrmacht Report of 14 December 1942

(Excerpt)

In other areas of the southern sector of the front, the sometimes very intense battles against the powerful enemy forces continue.

Our panzer forces, which advanced from the area south-west of Stalingrad, defeated strong enemy forces, whose counterattack collapsed with losses of over 20 armoured vehicles. During an advance that took place in recent days in the Kalmyk steppe, into the enemy's rear, numerous prisoners were captured, and the enemy's supply line was seriously disrupted.[5]

14 December 1942
The Battles at Verkhne Kumski
Map 8

Provided below are all radio messages available to this author to and from Battle Group Hünersdorff in the eventful days starting on 14 December 1942. They are presented here in sequence to document each event. They provide a valuable insight into the manner of leadership during the movements that were to follow.

Battle Group Hünersdorff Radio Traffic

0500hrs. Radio Message to I/11th Panzer Regiment

Deploy motorcycle reconnaissance to Gromoslavka, Shabalinski, and Novo Aksaiski. Scout routes to Shestakov, both direct and via Hill 146.9. Majority of Hünersdorff to assemble across the bridge at an estimated time of 0530hrs.

0510hrs. Radio Message to Division

Events during the night: two surprise fire attacks with Stalin's organs from the west. Command post Hünersdorff hit – seven wounded, several motor vehicles destroyed. In Verkhne Kumski it is quiet. Hünersdorff to assemble majority of troops after the completion of the bridge at 0530hrs.

War Diary of 11th Panzer Regiment

The mission for 14 Dec 1942 reads:

Hold the bridgeheads, provide reconnaissance at Gromoslavka, Shabalinski, and route reconnaissance toward the west and east.

The regimental commander further orders:

After completion of the bridge over the Aksai, Group Remlinger[6] (I/4th Panzer Grenadier Regiment minus one company – the one in Verkhne Kumski – with I/76th Artillery Regiment, 8th Company/Anti-Aircraft Training Regiment, 1st Company/41st Panzjäger Battalion, and one 8.8 Anti-Aircraft Battery) are to hold the bridgehead.

Group Küper[7] (II/114th Panzer Grenadier Regiment, minus 5th Company), 6/76th Artillery Regiment and two platoons of 2cm anti-aircraft guns, and 5/11th Panzer Regiment will be assigned to Oberst Unrein for special missions.

Staff/11th Panzer Regiment with II/11th Panzer Regiment, 5/114th Panzer Grenadier Regiment, 3/4th Panzer Grenadier Regiment, 10/Anti-Aircraft Training Regiment, one platoon heavy anti-tank guns, 2/41st Panzerjäger Battalion, and III/76th Artillety Regiment (minus 6th Battery) are to go to Verkhne Kumski, after completion of the bridge across the Aksai.

The new bridge was not completed in the expected time and during the night, it was repeatedly destroyed by enemy fire on Salivski, which brought further delays.

War Diary of 11th Panzer Regiment

0700hrs.

Bridge completed at 0600hrs. After two companies from II/11th Panzer Regiment had finished crossing, an attack by enemy tanks from Hill 79.9 (2km north-west of Salivski) was reported.

The II/11th Panzer Regiment is deployed against them, one enemy tank destroyed, two others flee westward.[8] An attack led by Battalion Remlinger to secure the west flank of the bridgehead toward Vodyanski, north of the Aksai, stalls out amid unexpectedly strong enemy fire. Remlinger has to transition to defence, and during the day is attacked from the west, [at his positions] north and south of the river.

This was the opening move of the first day of the tank battle in the Kalmyk steppe, one that lasted almost three days – one of the largest and most brutal tank battles of World War II, a battle between 200 German panzers and 300 to 400 Russian tanks. This enormous number of armoured vehicles was engaged constantly and simultaneously on the battlefield, in an engagement that was almost entirely a tank battle. It ultimately ended in a tie, and it was only later that the German side gained the upper hand.

Next morning, when we failed to capture Vodyanski, it became clear that the Russians had not totally disappeared. In fact, it was just the opposite. We were attacked at Salivski by the two Russian infantry divisions positioned outside of Kotelnikovo and the remainder of the Russian IV Cavalry Corps, probably with support from parts of the Russian 3rd Tank Army. The 23rd Panzer Division was attacked as well, by what turned out to be troops from a mechanised Russian Corps that belonged to the now slowly gathering Russian 3rd Tank Army.

Battle Group Hünersdorff Radio Traffic

0735hrs. Radio Message from II/11th Panzer Regiment
Position 800m north-west of 79.9.

? hrs. Radio message from II/11th Panzer Regiment
Enemy clearing out of the ravine. One tank destroyed, two others fled.

0745hrs. Radio message to I/4th Panzer Grenadier Regiment
6th Company, II/11th Panzer Regiment will initially remain for security at Hill 79.9, then will be moved on to Verkhne Kumski.

In response to the constant calls for help from Group Remlinger, along with reports that the troops ordered from Remlinger – troops originally meant for Verkhne Kumski – were instead to be deployed at the bridge-head, the following order was issued:

> 0756hrs. Radio message to I/4th Panzer Grenadier Regiment
> Deployment of any elements meant for Verkhne Kumski is forbidden. Report continuously on which units have gone over the bridge.

To clarify the above order: despite the fact that Group Remlinger was hard pressed at Salivski and was requesting more forces, Oberst von Hünersdorff was determined to do his utmost to send the reinforcements to Verkhne Kumski, as originally planned. He was fully certain that this is where the main battle would develop. The following radio message from the logistics commanders for the panzer regiment and the 41st Panzerjäger Battalion requests that the supply route be kept open, and at least not to order the anti-tank units back from their present positions west of Salivksi.

> 0810hrs. Radio Message from Squadron Borgs
> Panzerjäger south of the bridgehead engaging with enemy tanks

> ? hrs. Radio message from Squadron Niemann
> Niemann encountering enemy tanks south-west of Salivski.

> 0825hrs. Radio Message from 41st Panzerjäger Battalion
> At 0800hrs, two enemy tanks destroyed, 1km south of Salivski. According to statements by prisoners of war, tonight 20–30 enemy tanks moved into village 12km west of Salivski. Should self-propelled guns follow after or stay there for now?

> 0835hrs. Radio Message to 41st Panzerjäger Battalion
> Squadron should remain there for now.

War Diary of 11th Panzer Regiment

0900hrs.

At 0900hrs. the regimental commander arrives at Verkhne Kumski. At that same moment, Verkhne Kumski is attacked from the north by enemy infantry with several tanks. I/11th Panzer Regiment ordered to sweep around and counterattack frontally and to the west. Reconnaissance sent out from Verkhne Kumski provides no information concerning enemy tanks, but all further reconnaissance is prevented by encounters with enemy recon patrols, which are everywhere.

Battle Group Hünersdorff Radio Traffic

0940hrs. Radio Message to Division

Hünersdorff in Verkhne Kumski. Enemy presently advancing to Sogotskot and from out of the area of Verkhne Kumski north-eastwards with infantry and tanks. Counterattack initiated.

1020hrs. Radio Message to Division

1. According to motorcycle reconnaissance reports, between 0700 and 0800hrs., area south of Sogotskot is clear of enemy. Toward the north and north-east, no breaches. Five km south of Gromoslavka, two enemy scout cars. An engineer-officer states that in Gromoslavka, 300 tanks of all types. 10km south, 20 prisoners brought in.

2. Reconnaissance troops on Shabalinski, 9km north of Verkhne Kumski – two armoured reconnaissance vehicles and 20–30 riflemen. Recon troops had to turn around.

3. Reconnaissance troops on Novo Aksaiski report trench work 1.5km north-east of the village.

All this information taken together showed that the Russians were becoming active. In order to maintain our own freedom of action, Battle Group Hünersdorff decided to transition to the offence at two important locations – Salivski and Verkhne Kumski. Therefore, Remlinger – still under Hünersdorff's command – once more received the order to capture Vodyanski. Oberst Hünersdorff rejected the division's intention of supporting this attack with panzers from Verkhne Kumski, noting that he himself was battling strong enemy tank forces south of Verkhne Kumski. Group Remlinger, however, came upon a Russian counterattack and remained in position in front of the target just as he had been that morning.

1110hrs. Radio Message from Division
   If the Remlinger attack does not succeed and panzer support is not possible, bring the battalion back, hold the bridgehead with strong panzer defence, at least several panzers.

1431hrs. Radio Message from Division
   Defence group will be under command of Unrein for the time being.

1450hrs. Radio Message to Division
   Bridgehead must be ready and able to hold out against 18 enemy tanks.

But back to Verkhne Kumski. There, an exemplary report by the light platoon from II/11th Panzer Regiment showed new enemy tanks to the south-east of the village.[9] They would have to be dealt with as soon as I Battalion succeeded in defeating the enemy that had attacked from the north that morning. To exploit mobility and full firepower, the regimental commander decided to hunt the enemy in open terrain. For the II/11th Panzer Regiment, which had just arrived in the village a short time ago, this was their big moment.

War Diary of 11th Panzer Regiment

1200hrs.

According to prisoner-of-war statements, enemy tanks are in Sogotskot. The commander has decided to sweep around Verkhne Kumski from the south and attack these suspected tanks between Verkhne Kumski and Sogotskot. The commander, with II/11th Panzer Regiment and 4/11th Panzer Regiment, attacked at Hill 147.0 with their right flank (3km south of Verkhne Kumski) toward the east. After a short distance, the vanguard troops came upon enemy tanks. In a two-hour battle, in a heavy firefight, 32 enemy tanks were destroyed, with only two losses of our own.

Report
by
Commander, 6/11th Panzer Regiment

It was just after midday when the light platoon from my battalion (II) reported enemy tanks at Sogotskot. Our battalion mounted up immediately, and under the leadership of our commander, Major Dr. Bäke, we rolled out to face the reported enemy. West of the road leading to Salivski, using the terrain as cover, we headed southwards. After 4km, we turned eastwards, crossed over the road, moved in a broad wedge formation (two companies in front), and carefully advanced further. My company found itself forward to the right. We were to surround Sogotskot from the south, as from this area the light platoon radioed for help: they were being chased by T34s. We had barely gone about 2km east of the road, when we came to the top of a high flat ridge and came upon a surprising scene.

At a distance of nearly 1,000 metres stood a formation of about 40 tanks, painted white like ours, with black numbers painted on the turrets, their crews either outside the vehicles or sitting on them. This could not be the same enemy that had been reported by the light platoon. My first thought was that these were panzers from the 23rd Panzer Division The scene seemed far too German. But what were they doing in our sector? Then the riddle was solved: the barrels of the cannons were slightly too short. Also, the cupolas on the turrets appeared to be lacking. We rolled on aimlessly, debating back and forth by radio whether this was friend or foe. I nevertheless ordered my own panzer to aim in just in case it was the enemy, but to fire only if I, myself, fired a shot.

By now we were about 600m away, all nerves on edge, when over there, the crews jumped into their tanks and two of them charged us. I was just able to call out 'attention' on the radio, when the command came in through the battalion's radio frequency almost simultaneously (one side of the radio headset set was for the company's panzers, the other for the battalion): *Russians! Fire at will!*

But before a shot fell from our side, both advancing enemy tanks fired on us. They fired on the move, and despite the mere 300m between us, hit nothing. They were sacrificing themselves for nothing, it seemed.[ii] But then roared a broadside – in the truest sense of the word – from the two companies positioned forward, with the kind of effect that very few can muster. Many of the men must have been watching through their sights as the two tanks furthest forward literally blew up into pieces. The rest was child's play. At a distance of 600m and less, even with a 5cm long tube panzer, every shot was effective. With our faster rate of fire and better training, we were flat out superior. Hardly anyone of them survived. Those who fled were stopped by the 7.5cm long barrel cannons of the heavy companies, even from a distance of over 1km. The last ones were forced into a trough and fired on as if on the target range. Thirty-two black smoke clouds rose into the clear winter air.[10]

---

ii   Translator's note: '*Winkelriede, ohne Sinn ...*' Author uses the term *Winkelriede* here, referring to a Swiss historical figure and his self-sacrifice for a larger cause.

After regrouping, the battalion moved to the north in order to pick up the light platoon believed to be there, and to hunt down reported enemy tanks. The crew members of the platoon were soon found, but could not be picked up until later, as the enemy tanks in front of Sogotskot fired on us. Darkness forbade any further pursuit. Guided by illumination rounds from I Battalion, we rolled back to Verkhne Kumski in complete darkness.

Report
by
Leutnant H. Kallfelz,
Platoon Leader, Light Platoon, II/11th Panzer Regiment

On 14 December 1942 at around 0930hrs, as commander of the reconnaissance platoon of II/11th Panzer Regiment, I received orders to report to the command post in Verkhne Kumski.

There I received the mission from the regimental commander, Oberst von Hünersdorff, to conduct reconnaissance to the east and north-east and report any possible enemy sightings. I was also assigned the regimental motorcycle messenger platoon for this mission.

We left the village shortly before 1000hrs., and soon reached an area with a great many ravines and had to move slowly. In one especially steep ravine, we incurred our first loss when one of my panzers slid and overturned. The crew suffered some light, some serious injuries. I sent a report by motorcycle messenger to the regiment, asking the commander to send the repair service troops.

After getting past the ravine, we arrived at the steppe and moved in a broad wedge formation in the direction of Sogotskot (Hill 114). After driving about 3km, I sighted an enemy tank convoy heading from north to south. There were about 40 to 50 tanks which, travelling in a line, moved forward rather slowly due to frequent stops. I reported this enemy immediately to the regiment. Because I stood out in the open steppe, the Russians sighted me quickly. As their interest in my vehicles grew, I waved a hand to them, by which they apparently assumed that we belonged to them – at any rate they turned off without firing on us.

Soon a radio message came in: 'Return to the starting point.' But since I saw more enemy movement in addition to these tanks, I considered it my duty to remain there longer and send a report to the regiment.

It was not long before I noticed a new enemy tank unit to my left, possibly even larger than the first, apparently headed for Verkhne Kumski. I reported this to the regiment. Just as I started to withdraw, a third unit appeared from the direction of Sogotskot, which like the previous one consisted of T34s, KV1s, and KV2s. At first the convoy moved south, following the earlier one, but later on turned more to the west. Its mission appeared to be to surround Verkhne Kumski from the south.

My long pause may have provided the regiment with valuable information, but now my own unit was in a very difficult position; I found myself practically in the midst of three very strong Russian tank convoys. The 2cm weapons were no match for the Russian 12.5, 10.5, and 7.62 cannons. A battle would be hopeless from the outset. I radioed my situation to the regiment and requested support.

In response, I was told that both battalions were already engaged in battle with enemy tanks. I therefore tried to move slowly in the direction of Verkhne Kumski, in the hope of finding terrain features for cover. Quite soon, however, we were discovered by enemy convoys from the north and came under fire. Six T34s and KVs turned off toward us; we had to engage. The motorcycle messengers assigned to me attempted to reach the village one by one; later, many of them came up missing. After the Russians had completely surrounded us, I concentrated my fire on the engine area of a T34 and set it on fire. I then ordered a dismount. We sought safety in a ravine, but there we came upon some Russians, who, although some of them were wounded, immediately fired on us. Because there were more of us, we were able to overwhelm them after a short firefight and take their weapons from them. In their midst I also discovered a woman in a first lieutenant's uniform, who, according to her statement, had been the commander of a tank that had apparently been destroyed in the battle at Verkhne Kumski.

Quite soon we were discovered by Russian tanks, and we had to flee further. Before us was another flat plain; in the midst of this hopeless situation, several crewmembers surrendered. At the end I had only one sergeant and one NCO with me. Because we had broken up into several groups, I could not see any of the others. Then three more Russian tanks appeared in front of us and began shooting. There was no place to take cover, and our black uniforms stood out against the snow, leaving us no other choice but to pretend to be dead. On my order, we threw ourselves to the ground and remained lying there without moving. We could tell that these tanks had stopped 100m away from us. The minutes passed, seeming like an eternity. Finally, a tank drove up to us very slowly, and then passed by us about three or four metres away. Then the second tank followed, then finally the third came by. This one came so close that we feared it would run us over. We could have grabbed onto his track. Hardly had they passed than we jumped up and took cover behind the last Russian tank and sought safety and cover in a nearby dune. Here we found more members of our unit who had also escaped. We had reached the end of our nerves, but we were no longer being hunted.

From there, we could see that two Russian vehicles remained standing near our deserted panzers. Behind us and to the south we heard sounds of battle, but our own troops were nowhere to be seen. It was not until three hours later that some German panzers appeared and, after a short firefight, destroyed the two Russian vehicles. I requested that these panzers remain with us until we had rescued our own panzers, but they were called away by radio. We then went to our panzers and found them nearly undamaged. Only a few cables had been ripped from the radio equipment. Apparently, the Russians had wanted to tow these panzers away intact. Soon I regained contact with the regiment. If the Russians had had the ability and intention, they could easily have listened in to all of the radio traffic.

It was not until dark that the German panzers from II Battalion came and picked us up. The panzers from my platoon that were still operational were either towed or driven in to Verkhne Kumski.

War Diary of 11th Panzer Regiment

1500hrs.

At early nightfall the battle has to break off. The regiment regathers and returns to Verkhne Kumski. Meanwhile, Verkhne Kumski is under enemy pressure. Two attacks by 20 to 30 T34s and KV1s must be fended off. Three T34s destroyed, first in the village at a very short distance, three others blown up by German panzer destruction troops (*Panzervernichtungstruppen*). In particular, Oberstleutnant Scharfe distinguishes himself here. For the regiment, the day is a complete success. Out of about 80 enemy tanks, 43 are destroyed, with only a few losses on our side. The bridgehead at Salivski is also holding out against strong attacks from the west (north and south of the Aksai). Orders for the following day: wipe out enemy still located in Verkhne Kumski.

Battle Group Hünersdorff Radio Traffic

1510hrs. Radio Message to Division
    Tank battle broken off at nightfall. Enemy fleeing north. 43 heavy enemy tanks destroyed.

1546hrs. Radio Message from 6th Reconnaissance Battalion
    Battle sounds south of Krugelyalzov. Presumed to be 23rd Panzer Division Wounded: two officers, 53 NCOs and soldiers.

1710hrs. Radio Message from Squadron Borges

Location 2km east of Salivski. Since 1300hrs, Salivski under strong enemy tank and artillery fire. Now ended. We are on the march to Verkhne Kumski and attempting to break through.

1717hrs. Radio Message from I Battalion/4th Panzer Grenadier Regiment (Remlinger)

After heavy defensive fighting against Russian attack on both riverbanks, after fall of darkness enemy repelled for the time being. Russian attempt to surround with T34s and infantry on our southern flank defeated. For the time being, all quiet.

? hrs.

No Luftwaffe activity. Reached Verkhne Kumski line. In Salivski: I/4th Panzer Grenadier Regiment (minus 3rd Company), 1/2 of 1/41st Panzerjäger Battalion, 57th Pioneers, 8/Anti-Aircraft Training Regiment, one heavy anti-aircraft battery, Group Küper (II/114th Panzer Grenadier Regiment (minus 5th Company).

In Verkhne Kumski: 11th Panzer Regiment (minus 5th Company), 4/6th Reconnaissance Battalion, 3rd Company/4th Panzer Grenadier Regiment, 5th Company/114th Panzer Grenadier Regiment, one platoon from 41st Panzerjäger Battalion, III Battalion/76th Artillery Regiment (minus 6th Battery), 10th Company/Anti-Aircraft Training Regiment.

Captured goods (not counting Remlinger): 43 tanks, three anti-tank guns, six lorries, one infantry battalion dispersed (50 dead) (Russian 235th Tank Brigade).

Our losses (not counting Remlinger): dead: one NCO, two soldiers; wounded: one officer (Leutnant Preisendanz), 10 NCOs, 13 soldiers.

Out of action: two panzers totalled, nine panzers damaged (some mechanical, some from shooting).

2109hrs. Radio Message from Remlinger (I/4th Panzer Grenadier Regiment)

Casualties at bridgehead: dead: one officer, seven NCOs and soldiers.

An eventful and victorious day. The Russian units that had recently entered the battle – believed to be from the enemy's 3rd Tank Army – prevented any further advance but were still unable to overpower our division's positions. Until fall of darkness, all hills gained were successfully held, and with high enemy casualties. The Aksai front solidified, and after the arrival of most of Unrein's group, would not become a dangerous hotspot in days to come. Furthermore, in the coming days, the 17th

Panzer Division would arrive (from Orel), meaning that a whole division would be positioned in the area between the Don and Salivski. Even with its low number of panzers, it was still combat effective, and its presence was reassuring. As for casualties, they remained in a low range, especially considering the tough battles of that day.

The 23rd Panzer Division was also able to hold its positions against reinforced enemy pressure on the Askai, east of the division, and further solidify its bridgeheads.

This overall situation brings up some interesting points regarding leadership practices, for instance:

1. The panzer battle took place in open terrain, and all panzers were retained despite all calls for help. Both contributed to the victory at Verkhne Kumski.
2. Group Remlinger was temporarily placed under command of Battle Group Unrein. This reduced Hünersdorff's span of control in Verkhne Kumski and placed Remlinger in a better position to receive help from Battle Group Unrein, which had meanwhile moved in closer to him.
3. The quick and unadorned situation reports, by radio, on the rear battle area from the logistics officers of Battle Group Hünersdorff.

It was now certain that in the days to follow, the Russians would focus their entire strength and effort on Verkhne Kumski, which, for them, was an uncomfortably far-forward area.

Wehrmacht Report
15 December 1942

> In the Volga-Don Region, the infantry and tank units defeated the enemy attacks in hard fighting. They inflicted high losses on the Soviets and destroyed 67 Tanks.... etc.

15 December 1942
The Panzer Battle at Verkhne Kumski
Map 9

Battlegroup Hünersdorff Radio Traffic

0025hrs. Radio Message from Niemann (logistics commander)
Bridge crossing only possible by towing (due to icy surface); therefore, requesting towing equipment.

0030hrs. Radio message from I/4 Panzer Grenadier Regiment (Remlinger)
Russians occupying Hill 79.9 at strength of about one company with three tanks – and this early in the morning they are sitting directly under my nose. Couldn't someone come in from the rear and knock them flat?

0045hrs. Radio message to Niemann (supply commander)
Anything not over the bridge, leave it where it is, put under bridge! What is north of the bridge, take with you.

0400hrs. Radio Message to Division, Morning Report
Night in Verkhne Kumski passed quietly. Supplies underway. March readiness at dawn. Task organisation and panzer situation as reported yesterday.

War Diary of 11th Panzer Regiment

Verkhne Kumski, 15 December 1942
The night is passing quietly. Scheduled reconnaissance reports strong enemy movement from the north toward Verkhne Kumski.

Battle Group Hünersdorff Radio Traffic

0530hrs. Radio Message from I/4th Panzer Grenadier Regiment (Remlinger)
Russians appear to be readying for battle with their *Schwerpunkt* at our southern flank. Can I count on a spoiling attack toward the enemy force mustering in front of my northern position?

0626hrs. Radio Message from Niemann (Logistics Commander)

Located eastwards of Salivski. Crossed stream with some elements. Trying to bring vehicles across stream one at a time. Since daybreak, Salivski under strong enemy bombardment.

0720hrs. Radio Message to Division
Enemy infantry and cavalry elements and a few tanks in ravine area north-east and north of Verkhne Kumski.

Scouting of terrain opportunities for flank and rear attack … [?] are made difficult by lack of anti-tank ammunition (1,500 rounds are missing). The Division 6th Column urgently needed.

0725hrs. Radio Message from 4th Panzer Grenadier Regiment (Unrein)
Tank attack on south-western portion (Salivski) successfully defended against. Several T34s confirmed destroyed.

0730hrs. Radio message from II/114th Panzer Grenadier Regiment (Küper)
How is situation there? We are stopping! Strong defensive battles here.

0745hrs. Radio Message from 4th Panzer Grenadier Regiment (Unrein)
Convoy traffic possible in northern direction in great depth. Railway in the southern part of Salivski from time to time under artillery and tank bombardment.

0752hrs. Radio Message from Niemann
The Salivski-Verkhne-Kumski road is not open. Able to guide vehicles across the stream under most difficult conditions. Oberstleutnant Herbert with me.

As predicted, the Russians did attack promptly on the morning of 15 December. But they made their appearance at Salivski, on the front that had been fortified by Battle Group Unrein during the night. They were fought off and suffered many losses.

During the quiet moments that settled over Verkhne Kumski during the night, the necessary resupply began to Battle Group Hünersdorff, which was in position there. But because of the frozen roads to and from Aksai and the constant artillery fire on the overpass and on large stretches of the supply highway, it could only be carried out to the smallest extent.

Reconnaissance had reported enemy forces moving in from the north and north-east, and Oberst von Hünersdorff decided to attack them again at first light with elements of his battle group, in open terrain, just as on the previous day.

War Diary of 11th Panzer Regiment

0800hrs.

Ordered by the division to destroy this enemy force, the commander decides to take the panzer regiment and the 5/114th Panzer Grenadier Regiment (SPW), sweep northwards, and strike at its flank. He leaves behind a defence force in Verkhne Kumski under command of Major Löwe, Commander I /Panzer Regiment 11, consisting of two companies of panzers – the II/76th Artillery Regiment, the 3/4th Panzer Grenadier Regiment, the 4/6th Reconnaissance Battalion and the available anti-aircraft guns.

The regiment attacks in a long assault line toward the right, breaking off at the end again and again, lengthening at the front, moving toward the north-west. The enemy resistance is tenacious, especially the strong and well camouflaged anti-tank force, which stands fast and inflicts heavy casualties on the regiment. Our commander is out front and personally urges the unit on, but the enemy is very strong, well camouflaged, and cannot be seen, and he is unable to develop the attack in a fluid manner.

Battle Group Hünersdorff Radio Traffic

0810hrs. Radio message from II/11th Panzer Regiment (Commander Major Dr. Bäke)
Bäke ready to march in 15 minutes.

0815hrs. Radio message from Unrein (Commander, 4th Panzer Grenadier Regiment)
Get going! We are standing fast on our own!

0822hrs. Radio message from II/11th Panzer Regiment
Bäke is on the way.

0830hrs. Message to Küper (Commander, II/114th Panzer Grenadier Regiment)[11]
Bravo, Küper! Pursue quickly!

0831hrs. Radio message to Bäke (Commander, II/11th Panzer Regiment)

Straight ahead, two of our own lorries set afire by enemy tanks. Get there fast.

0835hrs. Radio message from Unrein (Battle Group Commander at Salivski)

Everything here in good order. Bridgehead is holding. Herbert on return trip, a T34 blown up by tank destruction detail.

0843hrs. Radio message from I/11th Panzer Regiment (Löwe)
Request Bäke's position.

0845hrs. Radio message to Löwe
Three km north-west of west exit Verkhne Kumski.

0849hrs. Radio message from Bäke
Löwe asking me for panzers.[12]

0900hrs. Radio message from Bäke
Anti-tank guns everywhere, can't see them.

0902hrs. Radio message to Bäke
Then sweep around left at highest speed and surround them.

0904hrs. Radio Message from Bäke
Wils [Commander, 4/11th Panzer Regiment] reports nothing visible, nothing … [?] Request artillery fire on enemy position.

0906hrs. Radio Message to Bäke
Quickly forward with strong left flank.

0908hrs. Radio message from Bäke
Wils reports eight enemy anti-tank sighted.

0928hrs. Radio message from Löwe
From east, attack on Verkhne Kumski with over-battalion strength and enemy tanks.

0930hrs. Radio message from Löwe
What is Bäke's situation?

0932hrs. Radio message to Löwe
We are surrounding the enemy from left.

0955hrs. Radio message from Küper (II/114th Panzer Grenadier Regiment)
What is situation with 5/114th and cannon platoon? Report personnel and material losses. Is resupply needed?

0958hrs. Radio message to Küper
Answer not possible this second, in middle of fight.

1001hrs. Radio Message from Löwe
Where is Hünersdorff and what is intent?

1003hrs. Radio message to Löwe
We are surrounding enemy to left.

1005hrs. Radio message to Division
In the middle of heavy fight with enemy tanks north-west of Verkhne Kumski.

In the morning, with the enemy closing in from the north and north-east, the commander ordered five of the seven panzer companies that had remained in Verkhne Kumski – reinforced by a mechanised company – to counterattack. This enemy force, already very close to the village and familiar with the German positions, could not – as it had been on the previous day – be taken by surprise. The battle began from a long distance away. Due to the enemy's poor optics and perhaps scant training, the German side did not suffer great losses. One problem was the supply vehicles which had not returned, as a battle over this village could be expected. Under orders to return immediately, they were forced to run the gauntlet. The question remains as to why the Russians closed only the village entrances and exits and left the road between Verkhne Kumski and Salivski open, although this would have been easy to block.

Because the fronts and positions shifted quickly during the running tank battle, the ability to provide artillery reinforcement was very limited. This was why it was of little use in the area north-west of Verkhne Kumski. Amid the interweave of fronts and the breadth of the battlefield, any outside observer would have had problems distinguishing friend from foe.

A more detailed description is provided in the following:

Report
by
Commander, 6/11th Panzer Regiment

On the morning of 15 Dec., in heavy fog, the village of Verkhne Kumski came under continuous and increasingly heavy tank, mortar, and machine gun fire, yet the enemy remained out of sight. The fires came predominantly from the north and north-west. Information gathered from reconnaissance troop and sector reports, as well as reports from the vehicles returning from the drive to Salivski which had suffered enemy bombardment, soon made it clear that the enemy was advancing toward the village, not just from the north, but from other directions as well.

On orders from the battle group commander, Oberst von Hünersdorff, the 1st and 2nd Companies of the panzer regiment, as well as the other elements of battle group in the village, were to remain in the village under command of Major Löwe, commander of I/11th Panzer Regiment Meanwhile, 3rd, 4th, 6th, 7th, and 8th Panzer Companies and one mechanised company from II/114th Panzer Grenadier Regiment were to break out toward the west, penetrate the enemy ring around the village, then pivot around the village northwards and overrun the enemy from the side. Simultaneously, the supply vehicles, other easily damaged elements of the battle group, and non-combat personnel were ordered to head for the less-threatened Salivski through the opening that had been made earlier.

Initially everything went as planned. The Russians retreated from our heavy panzer strike. Today I can still see Oberst von Hünersdorff, as we formed up for the break-out and rolled past him. In all his winter gear he stood at the turret of his command vehicle and to each commander he called out encouragement:

'Scheibert, get on it now; show what you can do!' I heard him yell out to me.

We soon reached open terrain. Looking back, I saw the supply lorries and other wheeled vehicles scattered far apart, disappearing at high speed behind the gently rolling terrain. The drivers in their unarmoured cabs had my sympathy. But under our protection, almost all were able to reach the protection of the village of Salivski. Only a few fell prey to enemy tanks and anti-tank guns.

After turning off and reassembling our four companies, we nevertheless understood that we faced a strong enemy, a foe whom we could not surprise and one who could take us under fire at long distances. The distances were too great for our 5cms to score any kills. To have any effect on a T34, we would have to be under 1,000m away. Thus, in the first phase of the battle, only the heavy (4th) Company with its 7.5cm cannons could score any kills. Aware of this situation, the battle group commander ordered the heavy company (8th Company), which was still in the village, to follow after us. On the other hand, we tried again and again to surround the enemy in a pincer movement, but each time, the enemy was always a step ahead. What developed was a lopsided front, one that wandered slowly toward the north-west, which, after incorporating 8th Company, had a width of about 8km. Finally, a ravine (north of Hill 95.6) prevented any further extension toward the left.

Amid losses on both sides, we initially succeeded in pushing the enemy back, but soon enough we found ourselves facing a heavy anti-tank force that completely showered us with salvo fires. The Russians worked according to a system of which they were the proven masters. It appeared that every tank towed an anti-tank gun, and initially the crew would be riding on the tank. When taking fire, they jumped off and acted as an infantry force. When the German defence grew too strong for their tanks, they hooked up their anti-tank guns and moved back under the protection of the tanks. Then they either created a new formation or tried to surround us from the other side. It was this game that we faced over again, in which their anti-tank guns grew increasingly miserable to deal with. In comparison, the Russian tanks were smaller targets than ours, they were almost invisible due to good camouflage, and they shot better than our panzers.

So it went, back and forth all morning. If we obscured the Russian tanks in order to quickly move in for a more favourable shooting distance, by the time the smoke lifted we would find ourselves facing a most unpleasant anti-tank front. When we managed to set a Russian tank or two on fire – due mostly to the work of our heavy companies – these successes only brought us losses and no victories worth mentioning. The entire horizon to the north and east was filled with Russian tanks and anti-tank fronts, yellow muzzle flashes lit the air, and everywhere clouds of black smoke hung over burning panzers, within both their lines and our own. It was like a sea battle, with a series of attacks followed by withdrawals, so vast in scale that an overall perspective was not possible. Much anti-tank fire was quieted by high explosive fragmentation shells, yet the Russians appeared to have inexhaustible reserves. It was clear that the 3rd Russian Tank Army was in full deployment against us. By radio came the most drastic attack orders, and again and again either Oberst von Hünersdorff, Major Dr. Bäke, or our personal commitment led us to the enemy; all the while our ammunition grew scarcer, and in the end, we were only using high explosive fragmentation shells.

It was a chaotic scene, with about 100 German panzers including the ones in Verkhne Kumski against about 300 Russian tanks and countless anti-tank weapons. The snow whirled around us; enemy rounds left long black streaks on the white steppe. Between our frequent changes of direction and the uniformity of the terrain, we had lost all sense of compass points. I could only sense my neighbours. From the light of the flares, I could now and again determine where my commander was located. Companies enmeshed with one another, and at long ranges vehicle identification was sometimes difficult, and it seemed at times that we were bombarding our own side.

Because of our reports that ammunition was running dry, and Löwe's reports of heavy defensive battles in Verkhne Kumski, we were called back at around 1100hrs. and regrouped in a low, protected area about 3km west of Verkhne Kumski. I also had to leave behind some disabled vehicles from my own company, along with the leader of my 1st Platoon (Leutnant Bonke), although we were able to rescue the crew.

Between our position and the village, we could see unaided that the Russians were moving toward Verkhne Kumski in a thick convoy of tanks, anti-tank guns, and infantry, without being at all concerned with us, although we lay clearly within their sight range. It was bizarre. From the direction of the village came some sounds of battle. We were feeling emotionally crushed, nearly beaten, and had had no significant successes; and added to this was the image of a mass of Russians who would just not quit coming. Between anger and loss, despair and anxiety, we felt overwhelmed.

But in the meantime, what had happened in Verkhne Kumski?

Battle Group Hünersdorff Radio Traffic

1030hrs. Radio message from Löwe
Request for immediate help. Enemy is in front of the village with 20 to 30 tanks.

1050hrs. Radio Message from Löwe
Requesting permission to clear area. If no help soon, Verkhne Kumski cannot hold.

1110hrs. Radio Message from Löwe
Now also under attack from the north. Request permission to clear out of the village, moving toward the west.

1120hrs. Radio Message to Löwe
Stand fast. We're coming!

1135hrs. Radio Message to Division
Verkhne Kumski is under attack from all sides. Must break off battle in order to relieve Verkne Kumski.

1150hrs. Radio Message from Löwe
Extreme emergency! Enemy in the village! When is Bäke getting here? We can't hold out much longer.

1200hrs. Radio Message to Division
Verkhne Kumski lost, attacking despite little ammunition.

1300hrs. Radio Message from Division
If Verkhne Kumski can't hold, clear out and return to bridgehead, hold bridgehead at any price.

1320hrs. Radio Message to Division
Verkhne Kumski retaken. Clear out as per orders, due to lack of ammunition.

1435hrs. Radio Message from Division
Is it possible to hold Verkhne Kumski if ammo is replenished?

1435hrs. Radio Message to Division
Verkhne Kumski is already vacated as per orders.

War Diary of 11th Panzer Regiment

1100hrs.

Just at the moment the enemy appears to be weakening, Major Löwe reports attacks from the east on Verkhne Kumski by some twenty T34s.

At 1110hrs. Löwe reports: 'Now under attack from the north as well. Request permission to move out of the village to the west.' Bäke, on the other hand, went into battle not fully resupplied with ammunition, now reports lack of ammunition due to the heavy expenditure; therefore, the commander decides to cease the attack and return to Verkhne Kumski to support Löwe, who is under threat. At 1120hrs., Remlinger reports new heavy attacks by tanks from the north against the bridgehead, and that the resupply route to Salivski is disrupted. Löwe reports breach by Russian forces into the village, and his calls for help more urgent.

1200hrs.

After a short halt in the advance, the commander attacks from the west in a broad wedge, despite lack of ammunition. Thanks mainly to his decisive, high-speed attack, he wins the battle quickly and retakes the village which had previously been lost, except for a group of houses in which Löwe had stopped with the remainder of his forces.

Report
by
Commander, 6/11th Panzer Regiment
continued ...

... Then two things happened that brought us back to life. First, Oberst von Hünersdorff arrived in his panzer right in the middle of us all, pulled his headset angrily from his head and roared at us. This is the only way to describe it:

'This is supposed to be my regiment? You call those attacks? This is a day of shame.' And so forth.

We were quite irritated about this talking-to, no matter how well we knew and loved his tough manner. Although we respected him greatly, not least because of his personal commitment, we believed he was treating us unfairly. He had been our commander for too short a time to be able to pass such judgment on us.

Major Dr. Bäke, commander of II/11th Panzer Regiment defended us, but the tension remained in the air, and our anxiety grew visibly.

The second thing that happened was the repeated urgent call for help from Major Löwe, commander of I /11th Panzer Regiment, from Verkhne Kumski which brought us to our next task.

Anyone who knew the old warrior, Major Löwe, knew this radio message was serious. If he had thought there was the smallest chance of holding Verkhne Kumski, not one call for help would have passed his lips.

Oberst von Hünersdorff and Major Dr. Bäke immediately called us commanders together, briefed us on the situation, and ordered us to break through into Verkhne Kumski on the double, at all costs.

It was a matter of freeing our regimental comrades, clearing the village of enemy, and rescuing all wounded. For this, the few panzers that still had ammunition were to take the lead, and the remaining panzers with the still abundant machine gun ammunition were to shoot wildly in hopes of creating panic.

And so it happened that Major Dr. Bäke led us forward. Two companies in front, three behind. The tank tracks kicked up snow, which swirled around us; we were in a wild mood, and if it had made any sense at that moment, we would have shouted *Hurrah!* We shot at every target that presented itself and as long as the machine guns lasted. Any Russian tank that stood up to us was shot by our lead vehicles, using rounds that the crews had saved up for this moment. Russian infantry fled in all directions, probably thinking us insane. But we succeeded, and in a very short time we were in the village, and as best I remember, without casualties. My only terrifying moment was when several T34s suddenly appeared to my right from a depression in the terrain at about 200 metres. I saw them direct their guns at me, but having no ammunition, I sat in the turret expecting to be shot any second. Then the vehicle closest to me was hit by a 7.5cm round on the front of the turret, so that it just lit up. It immediately rolled backwards and disappeared into the ravine. When the next one caught fire, the others turned back.

Soon we were in the middle of the village, and there we found the staff of I/11th Panzer Regiment Almost every officer was wounded, and all around us were burning panzers, both ours and Russian, sometimes standing nose to nose. I was ordered by Major Bäke to proceed to the eastern edge of the village. Every house was on fire. In the streets all around us lay the dead and wounded. Reaching the eastern edge of the village, I saw Russian infantry fleeing up the slope on the opposite side. In between times, we pursued with our machine guns. From the hills to the east several Russian tanks fired on the village. We could not touch them as we had no ammunition left.

From the impacts and metallic pinging on the armour of our vehicles, we knew we were still being fired on from some of the buildings around us. Not far away I saw two German wounded lying in a gulley, who beckoned to me with feeble hands. I thought about how I could rescue them and take them with me without placing others in danger, when my gunner pointed out to me that to my left, the company commander of 1st Company, HauptmannHoffmeyer, was attempting to rescue wounded men. He was on foot, as his vehicle had probably been shot. I tried to get his attention, but then he made a leap into the village road, fatally wounded, and collapsed. Seeing this approach wasn't going to work, I called other panzers from my company and formed a square as a shield against enemy fire. In this manner I succeeded in retrieving these and other wounded. Due to the extra human cargo, we could barely move in the turret. A short time later, a Panzer IV came up alongside (7.5cm, long) and took out an enemy tank on the eastern hill. From the number, I recognised the command panzer of 4th Company. As empty shells were being thrown from the side ports in the turrets. I recognised Hauptmann Wils, who waved to me, apparently having also recognised my panzer's number.

We continued firing to give the troops behind us the chance to rescue anything that could be rescued. The Russians were once more on the attack, having recovered from their earlier shock. Suddenly, however, the Panzer IV turned off and drove back into the village. Later I discovered that during another round of discarding empty shells, Hauptmann Wils had been killed by an incoming burst of fire.

Meanwhile, the other vehicles and the grenadiers in the mountain of wounded had not been idle; I received orders to slowly return to the west side of the village, as I would not have been able to remain standing still for long with no ammunition. As I appeared with my company at the point where we had broken through, I was confronted with a sad image.

The entire Battle Group Hünersdorff stood ready for the break-out to Salivski. At the head was one combat ready company, behind it the ambulance vehicles loaded with lightly wounded, followed by the infantry SPW, behind whose armoured plates lay the seriously wounded. At the end was 8th Company, commanded by Oberstleutnant Ranzinger. I transferred wounded men from my company, still hidden, to the group of wounded men. I was then ordered to take 8th Company and stall the Russians as long as possible, and to blow up and destroy anything that could fall into their hands. We were allowed several minutes so that we could provide cover to one another long enough fill our tanks with the remaining stored fuel and to pull the little ammunition that remained from the disabled tanks.

War Diary of 11th Panzer Regiment

On orders from Division, we vacate the village according to plan. Group Hünersdorff retreats southwards under the cover of darkness in order to conserve materiel. The day cost the regiment many lives.

Two officers dead, four officers wounded, one officer missing. Especially hard is the loss of Hauptmann Hoffmeyer and Hauptmann Wils, both of whom fought with high valour to the end.

Breaking off from the enemy goes relatively well. Although the route was bombarded from the west, we succeed in bringing the supply convoys and the drivable panzers back to Salivski. An attack by enemy tanks and infantry at the bridgehead in the evening is repulsed.

Radio Messages

1600hrs. Radio Message to Division, Daily Report

Assets Report: 23 enemy tanks hit, several anti-tank guns destroyed. Enemy infantry incurred heavy losses.

Our Losses: [13] dead: two officers (Hauptmann Hoffmeyer, Hauptmann Wils); 17 NCOs and soldiers; wounded: four officers (Major Löwe, Oberstleutnant Heesen, Oberstleutnant Berghes, Stabszahlmeister [staff pay master] Röchter), 20 NCOs and soldiers; missing: Oberstleutnant Ernsting. [14]

Hünersdorff still unhurt, panzer badly shot up.

Requests: requesting suitable commander for I/11th Panzer Regiment.

Suggestion: Hauptmann Glässgen.

Panzer Report: 6/21/7/5/2. [15]

Out of service for mechanical issues: 5.

Total out of service: one Panzer II (2cm), 13 Panzer III (5cm), five Panzer IV (7.5cm).

Report on the Retreat
by
Commander, 6/11th Panzer Regiment

At nightfall the long convoy began to move. I had to stay in the village until the vanguard reached certain points in the process in the march back to Salivski. I was then picked up by 8th Company, which was running security further to the rear at Hill 147.0. There I remained, my cannons pointed to the rear, until the company that I was to follow had rolled past me about 3km in the direction of Salivski and waited for me again. In this manner we provided cover for one another.

After the vanguard of the convoy had got through the ring around Salivski, I finally received orders to follow after them in a convoy. Incomprehensibly, the enemy did not pursue us – I still only had contact while in the village – so that I was able to keep to the schedule and break away from the enemy.

It was not until just before Salivski, in total darkness, that we ran into problems. From both right and left of the road, mostly from the right (west) side, came flashes of light. Not 400m away stood Russian tanks, which had probably heard the noises from our tank tracks and were creating a defensive barrier. They didn't trust themselves to come any nearer, however, and without any vehicle being affected by the illumination flares that sizzled around us, I reached Salivski at lightning speed. It was also probably eerie for the Russians. Barely had we arrived when we were immediately deployed as security at the bridgehead's front. Along with 8th Company, my defence sector was the west part of Salivski.

We didn't have to wait long, for soon we had T34s in front of us. In the light of the grenadiers' flares, we could see no more than 200 metres in front of us. Their winter camouflage flashed bright white. Two of them were immediately set on fire when the firefight began. Then attack after attack went on, all night long. In the light of burning houses and haystacks, we fought the Russians off repeatedly. We were no longer short on ammunition, so on this night, the cannon bores barely cooled down.

A hard day for the regiment. What had become perfectly clear was that the German Panzer III (5cm, long) was no match for an enemy that was attacking mostly with T34s. That day we saw that with panzers alone, any forward progress against this opponent was not going to be possible. We would have to go at him systematically with artillery and air support. Reports to this effect were sent to the senior office, the LVII Panzer Corps under command of General of Panzer Troops Kirchner.

Verkhne Kumski was lost. Had the Russians decided more quickly, and if they had gone after our retreat lines to Salivksi, which they absolutely could have done, it would have meant catastrophe for Battle Group Hünersdorff, which had almost no ammunition.

And so, despite all the losses, the combat vehicles that had meanwhile been put back into service amounted to about 100 panzers. Here around Salivski was enough artillery to spoil any Russian attacks. To remain on the defensive with these forces was contradictory to the mission and tactics of the German commanders.

So the decision was made to launch a renewed panzer raid only two days later in the direction of Verkhne Kumski in conjunction with the panzer forces of the 23rd Panzer Division (201st Panzer Regiment). The next day (16 December 1942) was set for fortifying the front at Aksai, and establishing contact with the 23rd Panzer Division, leaving the Russians on their own for the time being.

Wehrmacht Report of 16 December 1942

(Excerpt)

Between the Volga and Don, German and Romanian troops stormed several well defended villages, fiercely defeating counterattacks.

16 December 1942
Fortifying the Aksai Front
Map 10

War Diary of 11th Panzer Regiment

Salivski, 16 December 1942

The intent for the 16th is: hold the bridgehead while Group Unrein attacks the enemy at his western flank at Vodyanski. This is to neutralise the threat to our flank.

Regiment leaves for the hill 2km north of the bridge and arrives after a short battle with enemy tanks, during which two are destroyed. At 1200hrs., enemy sends reconnaissance from the north to scout out the situation. From the west, 10 tanks attack with riflemen, which were fought off after a hard battle, during which four T34s, nine anti-tank guns were destroyed. We made contact with our neighbour to the right, the 201st Panzer Regiment, and set up communications. Our reconnaissance reports strong enemy position with anti-tank guns on Hill 147.0. At nightfall the regiment is brought back to the starting position at the bridgehead.

During the commanders' conference in the evening, a renewed attack on Verkhne Kumski is ordered to take place in conjunction with the 201st Panzer Regiment We are to take Verkhne Kumski from the west. Leaving at 0500hrs, we advance from Klykovo toward the east as far north as Shestakov. From there, we turn north, onto divided road through the Neklinskaya ravine as far as the intersection 1km west of Hill 146.9. Here we are to turn off to the west, capture the enemy field positions on Hill 147.0 from their flank and rear, and capture Verkhne Kumski from the west. No other approaches to the village have proven to be possible for German panzers.

Battle Group Hünersdorff Radio Traffic

0645hrs. Radio Message to Division
  Assembled at the hill 2km north of the bridge.

0800hrs. Radio message to Division
  Established communications with Heydebreck (Commander, 201st Panzer Regiment).

1200hrs. Radio Message to Division
  Destroyed anti-tank gun position with four T34s, nine anti-tank guns (including one 7.62)[iii] and eight lorries. Our losses: three tanks (one totalled).

Report on the Retreat
by
Commander, 6/11th Panzer Regiment

The morning of 16 December found us in an attack that had been well prepared by our artillery. Amid very high enemy losses, we pushed as far as 2km forward and secured the area from a high elevation point with a clear overview of the

---

iii Translator's note: 76.2 in American and British nomenclature.

steppe. From these positions, over the course of the day, we were able to perform various missions.

During one of these raids, together with Hauptmann Gericke, commander of 7th Company, I stumbled on an anti-tank defence position. But the Russians were shooting so badly, that with 7th Company's fire support, I dared a frontal attack. I got my track guards shot off, and two other panzers of my company were damaged, with the vehicle of Uffz. (Sgt.) Pöttgen losing half of his cannon mantlet, sending shards flying. But despite the damage, we reached the enemy in a quick, final pass and overran him. After we had driven through all the defensive nests and had shot into their openings, I jumped behind some panzers (we were held under fire from a Russian position to the north-west). That day I found an undamaged Jeep – an American make, tied it to my panzer and towed it behind me. Later on, I had a great deal of fun with it.

Slowly, all grew quiet. Apparently, the Russians had pulled back their units for recuperation. The great panzer battle ended with no decisive win, either way. As it turned out, few of the enemy tanks had followed us as we left Verkhne Kumski; we had always met the Russian attacks with a sharp rebuff, and moreover, their attacks had also lost their previous toughness. Careful estimates indicated that in the past days the Russians had a total of 180 tanks completely destroyed from both tank divisions at the front. In the same time period, our regiment had 21 totalled tanks, with all others back in combat condition after a few days.

Battle Group Hünersdorff Radio Traffic

1415hrs. Radio Message to Division

At nightfall, I am taking panzers back to the perimeter of Salivski village and leaving combat outposts on the hills. Re-occupying at daybreak unless ordered otherwise.

1600hrs. Radio Message to Division (6.)[iv]

We reached the ordered objective, the hills 3km north of the bridgehead, after a short battle against enemy tanks on both riverbanks. Enemy deployed reconnaissance from the north with tanks, and from the west, attacked with 10

---

iv   The (6.) is in the original.

tanks and riflemen. He was beaten back having lost four T34s, nine anti-tank guns, and eight lorries. Along with the 201st Panzer Regiment, 3km north-west of 'W', in the morning, communications established.[16] At nightfall the infantry combat outposts left at map contour line, while the majority of the reinforced regiment spent the night providing security directly on the perimeter of the village. Command post Hünersdorff in Salivski.

Enemy assessment: majority of the enemy with numerous tanks at Verkhne Kumski. Security at the map contour line both sides of 147.0.

The 16th of December was a relatively quiet day except for the expansion of our bridgehead to the north, and the various forays by our panzer forces starting from that line; the time was used to repair and deliver restored panzers, which meant every company returned to a reasonable fighting strength.

It was surprising to note that the stronger Russian tank units showed little activity and did not make an appearance.

During the course of the afternoon, the commanders' conference took place as was mentioned in the War Diary. During this time the weaker 201st Panzer Regiment, under command of Oberstleutnant von Heydebreck and reinforced by several other units from the 23rd Panzer Division, was placed under Battle Group Hünersdorff. Orders were issued for the combined advance on 17 December. The order is shown below in its original form:

Orders Issued

Battle Group von Hünersdorff   16 Dec 1942

To
Regiment Heydebreck

Heydebreck, supported by an SPW battalion, one artillery battalion, and one heavy anti-aircraft battery is assigned to Hünersdorff. On 17 December at 0500hrs. Hünersdorff will advance from S. [Salivski], by way of K.O. [Klykovo-East], to the east section of the Neklinskaya ravine, on the southern slope of Hill 146.9; from there they are to advance west, destroy the enemy tanks positioned south of Verkhne Kumski, and take Verkhne Kumski from the west.

Simultaneously, the reinforced 6th Reconnaissance Battalion from S. [Salivski] will advance northwards to tie down the tank forces positioned south of Verkhne

Kumski. After the capture of Verkhne Kumski, Hünersdorff's mission is to go around Sogotskot from the east, advance to Gromoslavka, capture it, and hold open the bridge across the Myshkova river for the units that will follow.

Heydebreck will hold open the passage either across, or east, of the Neklinskaya ravine for Hünersdorff and in this manner will be placed in front of Hünersdorff.

The routes of advance, through and east of the Neklinskaya, will be scouted well in advance, along with reconnaissance in the direction of Gromoslavka.

As of 0515hrs., signallers must stand ready to guide most of Hünersdorff.

I will be in S.[Salivski] as of 0500hrs. at the head of the main body of Hünersdorff.

signed v. Hünersdorff

With Stuka support arranged, and the 17th Panzer Division finally assembled, a major advance in the direction of Generalovski was planned for 17 December. This would relieve the threat to 6th Panzer Division's left flank, and allow Group Zollenkopf, at this time still positioned south of the Aksai, to be released for other missions. The following days promised to be more successful.

Wehrmacht Report of 17 December 1942

(Excerpt)

In attacks supported by combat air units, German and Romanian troops pushed the enemy further back between the Volga and Don. At the large bend of the Don river, they fought off repeated attacks from strong forces, sometimes in counterattacks, and destroyed some 30 Soviet tanks.

17 December 1942
The First Failed Attack on Verkhne Kumski
Map 11

War Diary of 11th Panzer Regiment

0800hrs.

The departure is delayed for about one hour, as Heydebreck Regiment is not ready on time. At 0620hrs. the first enemy contact takes place north of Shestakovo, where enemy tanks have broken through at the bridgehead of the 23rd Panzer Division At 0715hrs., after destroying six enemy tanks, the advance continues. One company from Heydebreck is left behind in Shestakovo to mop up, and four enemy tanks are destroyed there with no losses to our side.

Battle Group Hünersdorff Radio Traffic

0525hrs. Radio Message to our Battle Group
Fall in.

0530hrs. Radio Message from Division
Attention! Enemy tanks from the north-west at Shestakovo.

0550hrs. Radio Message from Division
40 enemy tanks from Shestakovo heading west.

0550hrs. Radio message to Division
Hünersdorff has reached Klykovo.

0603hrs. Radio Message to Division
Further advance from Klykovo delayed because Heydebreck hasn't left yet.

0620hrs. Radio Message from Division
Enemy tanks have broken through into Shestakovo from north.

0650hrs. Radio Message to Division
Enemy tank advance from north, in area 2km east of Klykovo fended off. So far two T34s destroyed.

0712hrs. Radio Message from Heydebreck
So far six enemy tanks destroyed.

0725hrs. Radio message to Division
Are any of our troops remaining in Shestakovo? Otherwise, Stukas.

0728hrs. Radio Message to Division
Turn around at Hill 66.5km east of Klykovo, and head north.

0805hrs. Radio message to Division
Start of fighting directly south of Neklinskaya ravine. At hill north of this, enemy tanks sighted. In Shestakovo, still fighting. One of Heydebreck's companies mopping up. So far 10 enemy tanks destroyed. Pushing further north.

0806hrs. Radio Message from Heydebreck
Arrived at Neklinskaya ravine.

0810hrs. Radio Message from Division (Response to radio message at 0725hrs.)
In Shestakovo, infantry of neighbour [23rd Panzer Division].

An enemy counterattack at the bridgehead of 23rd Panzer Division was successfully fended off. The attack cost the Russians 12 tanks, but delayed our advance by two hours, which would prove painful later on.

The delay meant that we had to travel over the iced-over Neklinskaya ravine so as to save time, a long detour that made us more vulnerable to attack, which in turn, could divert us from the day's stated objective – Verkhne Kumski.

War Diary of 11th Panzer Regiment

1200hrs.

At 0850hrs. vanguard arrives at the road intersection 1km west of Hill 146.9 and comes upon a large enemy position with very strong tank defence and mines. The commander orders artillery to take positions and deploys II/114th Panzer Grenadier Regiment. At 0930hrs. the enemy position is captured, and the area is strewn with [Russian?] anti-tank rifles (about 50 are captured). The I/11th Panzer Regiment takes over direct fire protection against the enemy tanks that were reported to be north of the ravine (they proved later to be the ones already destroyed on 14 Dec.). At 1000hrs, [the unit] turns off to the west. At 1030hrs. II/11th Panzer Regiment takes over security of north flank, where several enemy tanks are also scouting. At 1150hrs, after a smooth forward advance, the group reaches Hill 147.0 on southern perimeter.

Battle Group Hünersdorff Radio Traffic

0820hrs. Radio Message to Division
With elements on north map contour line of the ravine. Icy march conditions, very difficult. Captured so far are six heavy mortars, two anti-tank systems, five lorries, and several machine guns.

0850hrs. Radio Message from Heydebreck
At Hill 146.9, enemy position with anti-tank rifles and mines. Request deployment of infantry and artillery, so that I can continue attack.

0900hrs. Radio Message to Küper [Commander, II/114th Panzer Grenadier Regiment]
Küper vacate enemy position at 146.9.

0910hrs. Radio Message from Division
Strong enemy supply traffic from Sogotskot to Verkhne Kumski (air reconnaissance report).

0920hrs. Radio Message to Bäke and Heydebreck
15 enemy tanks on advance from the west. Heidebreck and Bäke firefront.[17]

1000hrs. Radio Message to Division
Holding enemy at road intersection west of 146.9. Advancing *en masse* to attack toward the west.

1000hrs. Radio Message from Küper
Enemy anti-tank rifle position captured.

1020hrs. Radio Message from Division
5th Company/11th Panzer Regiment with seven tanks with Remlinger, will make contact with Hünersdorff along with Quentin [Commander, 6th Reconnaissance Battalion].

1026hrs. Radio Message to Bäke
Bäke, provide flank protection at road intersection, toward north.

1100hrs. Radio Message from Division
Kolchos 8.M. (Marta), large assembly of enemy motor vehicles.[v]

1150hrs. Radio Message to Division
Arrived 147.0.

Report on Retreat
by
Commander, 6/11th Panzer Regiment
Continued ...

... With elements of the 23rd Panzer Division, we attacked toward the north, avoiding Sogotskot, intending to retake Verkhne Kumski. Simultaneously the non-armoured elements pushed out from Salivski toward the same destination.

---

v   Kolchos 8.M. (Marta) = location code. (Marta = letter M.)

They were accompanied by the assault guns (*Sturmgeschütz*) that had been assigned them earlier by the division.

After early successes we ran across a strongly built-up defence position north of the Neklinskaya ravine. In shielding ourselves from this front, our attack had to head more to the west. With the help of the SPW battalion, we smoked out this position. At the same time, I/11th Panzer Regiment, along with the panzers of the 23rd Panzer Division, made a failed attempt to capture Sogotskot. Our advance was thwarted, just as it had been in Verkhne Kumski, by a whole system of defensive positions around the village. The position right in front of us also proved to be set up excellently. Very narrow and deep firing ports, occupied by a very tough enemy. No one surrendered, although we were located with the entire battalion in the middle of the enemy positions. The Russians would have to be shot out from their positions one by one. As the ground was thoroughly dug up, any driving back and forth had to be avoided so as not to throw a track.

Each panzer took on a certain share of firing ports which they had to monitor and wait for a Russian to appear from one of them. Peering out sideways through my observation slit, this was an eerie scene. The tanks stood like elephants with long stretched out trunks, as if sniffing at the earth. Finally, the infantry came with their SPWs and cleared out the entire system rather quickly under our protection. It was high time, too, because far off in the northern areas, the enemy tanks and anti-tank fronts, which were always better than us at aiming in, became uncomfortably visible. Our waiting panzers also offered an easy target, even for the worst anti-tank gunners.

After neutralising this position, we moved somewhat back into a reverse slope position, and re-joined the firefight. Meanwhile the artillery took on this anti-tank front, so we soon followed the other panzer units already positioned far to the west.

So, we took off, with security on our north side. Sogotskot lay before us, and we ran through our old battlefield of 14 December, with all of its derelict Russian tanks. We were still under constant fire, although we could never properly see the enemy at the village perimeter of either Sogotskot or Verkhne Kumski, We managed to arrive at the attack on Verkhne Kumski and had a second confrontation. The system of positions at the perimeter of the village, however, prevented us from breaking through. In addition to this, despite a preparation attack by the Stukas, the enemy defensive fire proved too strong. Enemy tanks appeared at our left flank and pulled us toward the north. Then as we drove through the battlefield of 15 December, darkness fell. Our burned-out panzers still stood there, but we could not rescue them. The Russians tried to cut off our line of retreat – this time they proved very clever, and we had to escape in total darkness, zigging and zagging as we went. As was frequently the case, we were guided by illumination flares from the south, thanks to the grenadiers from our division that had finally pushed forward halfway to Verkhne Kumski. The entire operation proved to be nothing more than a puff of air.

War Diary of 11th Panzer Regiment

1800hrs.

Due to terrain difficulties and the very slow clearing out of enemy positions at the road intersection, it is not possible to bring the infantry and artillery forward quickly enough. Because of the hour's delay, the commander decides to take full advantage of daylight, and attack Verkhne Kumski without infantry and artillery. The attack, now only supported by Stukas, runs into tough defensive fire and by 1350hrs. is fought off. During the attack, darkness falls. This night attack, which had been ordered by the division, promises little success due to the badly worn panzer forces and the fact that there is only one battalion, not to mention that there is little ammunition and fuel available. The commander therefore decides, with the consent of the division, to retreat and regroup on the south-east slope of Hill 147.0. Due to navigational challenges and darkness, the group does not arrive at the collection point until 1730hrs. It is not until 2100hrs. that the division orders the panzers to return to the original starting area.

Battle Group Hünersdorff Radio Traffic

1230hrs. Radio Order to I/11th Panzer Regiment
Careful attention at Kolchos 8.M.!

1300hrs. Radio Message from Division
Hill 147.0–137.2 occupied enemy positions.

1335hrs. Radio Message from Division
17th Panzer Division in battle for bridge at Generalovksi.

1335hrs. Radio Message to Himmelsbach [Löwe's replacement as commander of I/11th Panzer Regiment]
Leave the village [Kolchos 8.M.] alone! Your place is behind Heydebreck's left flank.

1345hrs. Radio Message to I/11th Panzer Regiment
Destroy enemy tanks and [?] at the left flank of Heydebreck!

1420hrs. Radio Message to Division
Our first attack on Verkhne Kumski was fended off by extremely strong anti-tank guns.

Stuka attack had no effect. Several panzers destroyed.

1445hrs. Radio Message to Division
Gathering west of Verkhne Kumski for another attack if it is still light enough.

1500hrs. Radio Message from Division
At 1400hrs. Quentin began advancing on Verkhne Kumski.

1520hrs. Radio Message from Division
Take the village with dismounted grenadiers under artillery and panzer protection.

1545hrs. Radio Message to Division
Due to darkness, attack will not be renewed. Group assembled at 147.0. Suggestion:

Return to start position and carry out resupply.

1600hrs. Radio Message to Division
Message from 1520hrs. not put through until nightfall. Night attack with only one battalion promises no success considering enemy strength.

1605hrs. Radio Message to Division
Decision requested as to whether night attack is to be carried out.

1630hrs. Radio Message to Division
Lost forward air control officer with radio station, as well as Heydebreck's radio station, from direct hit.[18]

1730hrs. Radio Message to Division
Renewed preparations undertaken at 147.0. Renewed tank attack not possible due to darkness. Strong occupation in Sogotskot, Verkhne Kumski and Kolchos 8.M.

1800hrs. Radio Message from Division
Location of panzers and both SPW battalions? [Author's note: 6th Reconnaissance Battalion also had SPWs some of the time.]

1855hrs. Radio Message to Division
Location is south-east slope Hill 147.0.

? hrs. Radio Message to Division (Day's Report)

Successfully repulsed a strong tank advance at Shestakovo with quick, determined action, throwing enemy back across Neklinskaya ravine toward the north, also capturing the hills north of there. After breaking through the very stubborn resistance from field positions at Hill 146.9 and west of there, we drove past Hill 147.0, always in a quick forward push toward the west, overrunning numerous anti-tank guns, and fighting off tanks. Then we launched enveloping attack from the west on Verkhne Kumski; our artillery was still not in place and the grenadiers remained behind; the tanks attacked in order to take full advantage of daylight. Due to extraordinarily strong defensive fighting, despite Stuka attacks, the Russians fended off our attack. During preparations for a renewed attack darkness fell. The preparations for a possible night attack on 14.7.0 were postponed in order to refuel and reload ammunition.

Captured/destroyed: 11 tanks destroyed, 15 lorries, one armoured reconnaissance vehicle (*Spähwagen*) destroyed, numerous infantry weapons captured, 10 anti-tank guns, 50 anti-tank rifles destroyed, six trench mortars (*Granatenwerfer*) destroyed, 100 prisoners of war brought in.

Out of service: 14 panzers, number of salvaged panzers undetermined, 10 SPWs.

Losses: Killed: forward air control officer, three NCOs and soldiers; wounded: 26 NCOs and soldiers.

This day of attacks – essentially unsuccessful attacks – had something to teach us. Regardless of the particulars of the enemy situation, it was now seen that a systematically constructed attack could cut a swath into this strong enemy. Working with combined arms against a tough, defensive enemy proved insufficient. Once more – as had happened earlier on the Aksai – an iced-over ravine hindered the arrival of supporting troops, so that even in daylight it was not possible to arrange a coordination of all weapons to face this most important target. It seems incomprehensible that the grenadier forces advancing north from the positions north of Salivski were unable to coordinate with the panzers that were coming from the east for their arrival at Verkhne Kumski. The very short Stuka attack, although helpful in its timely execution, showed little effectiveness against the deeply dug-in enemy.

Once more the Russians demonstrated their gift for digging-in very quickly and very deeply, even in the worst weather conditions (such as frozen ground). Furthermore, the Russian positions out in the middle of open terrain (e.g., road intersection 146.9) showed their preference for less-populated villages compared to the Germans, regardless of cold weather.

For 18 December, therefore, an artillery and air attack was ordered from positions near 147.0 on Verkhne Kumski. The panzer regiment was to break through into the village and attack the enemy in its weakened condition; on the same day they were also to capture bridges on the Myshkova river sector.

On this evening, Battle Group Hünersdorff presented a very sad appearance, both materially and physically. This is depicted in the last paragraph of the War Diary of 11th Panzer Regiment for 17 December.

War Diary of 11th Panzer Regiment

Because of the uninterrupted deployments of the past days, which have left no opportunity for maintaining vehicles, the deployment readiness of the regiment has sharply fallen. But also the crews, who since 11 Dec. have had no roof over their heads and barely any time to sleep, are much exhausted. Under these conditions, a renewed deployment on the next day promises little success, and in the opinion of the commander, will only cost an unnecessary loss of resources, which would be incommensurate with the goals that have been set, as has been demonstrated in the recent days.

Wehrmacht Report of 18 December 1942

(Excerpt)

Between the Volga and the Don, German divisions penetrated strongly held enemy positions on a dominating mountain range and by this attack gained further territory.

18 December 1942
The Second Failed Attack on Verkhne Kumski
Map 12

Battle Group Zollenkopf had been freed up when 17th Panzer Division took over their sector. Now it was they who were ordered to attack Verkhne Kumski, with support from other of the division's forces, including two panzer companies from 11th Panzer Regiment.

War Diary of 11th Panzer Regiment

Salivski, 18 Dec 1942

For today the panzer regiment remains available to the division, with orders to first penetrate the resistance, then pursue the enemy. The morning passes amid constant deployment preparations with technical service.

After Group Zollenkopf makes good forward progress, the regiment is ordered to the south-east slope of Hill 147.0, to be able to defend against the enemy tanks at the group's flank and rear. They move into the assembly area at 1230hrs. Against the objections of the regimental commander, during the night, the division orders two panzer companies to deploy as direct support for Group Zollenkopf, one on each flank. The two companies support the panzer grenadiers in an outstanding manner. But by 1200hrs., due to damage from anti-tank weapons, mines, and mechanical breakdowns, they are so weakened that the division requests they be sent back, especially because they shot up all their ammunition and only have two combat ready vehicles left.

The division makes it known that according to a wire-tapped Russian radio message, the defenders of Verkhne Kumski have been designated as guards by Stalin, a sign that the Russians, too, recognise the dangerous potential of our advance.

A deployment of the regiment will no longer be necessary today. After several requests by the commander for permission to bring the panzers back to the starting position for further maintenance, a retreat order is issued at 1750hrs. The panzer count is still 8/25/13/5/6. This means that now the entire regiment amounts to only one much weakened battalion. For the next day, however, there are still some panzers expected to come out of maintenance.

Battle Group Hünersdorff Radio Traffic

1200hrs. Radio Message to Division
Moved into assembly area east of 147.0.

1220hrs. Radio Message to Division
Request withdrawal of panzer support company (Panzerunterstützungskompanie) assigned to Hauschild, as only two vehicles and no ammunition are left.

1400hrs. Message from Division
Stalin has named the defenders of Verkhne Kumski as guards.

1510hrs. Radio Message to Division
Request permission to pull in for repairs at north boundary of Salivski, as no more opportunity to attack due to darkness.

1600hrs. Radio Message from Division
Wait for order, as termination situation is unclear.

1610hrs. Radio Message to Division (Daily Report)
Preparation for attack at 147.0, to prevent an enemy counterattack at the flank of Group Zollenkopf.

Panzer count: 8/25/13/5/6.

Losses: Dead: Oberstleutnant Böhm, one NCO.

Out of service: three Panzer IIIs.

1730hrs. Radio Message to Division (6.)[vi]

I consider any further waiting around here an unnecessary waste of resources and a serious disregard for maintenance.

1745hrs. Radio message from Division
Return to starting position.

1750hrs. Radio Message to Division
Retreating.

Despite all artillery support and various breaches into the exterior system of positions around Verkhne Kumski, we failed to capture the village. The enemy had brought forth all of his toughness and tenacity.

---

vi Parentheses (6.) in original

During the night the grenadiers remained close to the enemy, in the positions they had already taken, planning to spearhead a new attack next morning. Reinforcements were brought forward, air support authorised (Stukas), and the 17th Panzer Division was instructed by the corps to expand their bridgeheads across the Aksai at Generalovksi in the area of Kolchos 8.M., and west of there, on 19 December, eliminating a possible flank threat during the coming assault on Verkhne Kumski.

Battle Group Hünersdorff, consisting of the 11th Panzer Regiment and the SPW battalion, II/114th Panzer Grenadier Regiment, received the following mission for 18 December: capture Verkhne Kumski, and then pursue the retreating enemy as far as the Myshkova sector, without regard for the flank.[vii]

Wehrmacht Report of 19 December 1942

(Excerpt)

Despite tough resistance, German and Romanian troops threw the enemy further back toward the north-east, between the Volga and Don.

19 December 1942
The Breakthrough at Vassilyevka
Map 13

War Diary of 11th Panzer Regiment

On 19 December the attack by Group Zollenkopf continues. At about 1100hrs., we take Verkhne Kumski from the east and west. The grenadiers greatly benefitted from the attack by the panzer regiment from the 17th Panzer Division, which had joined them on their left.

The regiment, which launched its attack south-east of 147.0 yesterday at 0700hrs., is now in pursuit of the enemy on his northward retreat, as division believes enemy is wearing down.

---

vii Editor's note: this paragraph is placed as in the original book, though chronologically out of order.

1530hrs.

After advancing smoothly, hampered only by difficulties in terrain, the regiment is brought to a halt and ordered to turn off to the west. Regiment starts out again at 1320hrs., now ordered to cross the road intersection 1km west of 146.9, west of the Solenaya ravine to Vassilyevka, and to construct a bridgehead there. At 1440hrs., facing strong enemy positions north of the road intersection, they retreat. At 1525hrs., (Central European time) in the darkness, they overrun a strong anti-tank position south of the road intersection, and after a short battle, they are able to break through.

Battle Group Hünersdorff Radio Traffic

1222hrs. Radio Message to Division
    Not able to turn off to the right if I don't know where I am supposed to go.

[Author's note: This message came in response to division's orders to break off the advance by way of Verkhne Kumski and Sogotskot, and to pursue the enemy eastwards.]

1320hrs. Radio Message to Division
    Hünersdorff arrived at 146.9. Crossed road Sogotskot-Salivski.

1440hrs. Radio Message to Division
    From 146.9 to ravine 3km west of Sogotskot, strong position with dug-in anti-tank guns. In addition, eight tanks sighted so far. Turning south Hill 146.9.

1450hrs. Radio Message from Division
    23rd Panzer Division under strong attack at its bridgehead, coming from the direction of Shivkaya ravine southwards.

By order from corps staff, as long as there is no immediate flank threat, under no circumstances will Battle Group Hünersdorff be permitted to turn off and move south. Capturing the bridgehead of Vassilyevka is of crucial significance.

Group Zollenkopf is ordered to immediately release Battalion Hauschild, along with a battery and anti-aircraft gun, and have them follow Battle Group Hünersdorff. When Battalion Hauschild arrives, it will be placed under command of Battle Group Hünersdorff.

Regiment staff of 114th will also follow immediately and will place their two Panzer Grenadier battalions under command of Hünersdorff. Artillery will follow as soon as possible.

1455hrs. Radio Message to Division
Location west of 146.9 (3km). Taking fire from the south. Due to darkness, targets cannot be seen well.

1525hrs. Radio message to Division
Have broken through enemy position south of 146.9. Enemy retreating northward.

1605hrs. Radio Message to Division
Location 6km east of D (Hill 146.9).[19]

1645hrs. Radio Message from Division
Just keep on riding, 4th Husarenreiter.[20]

1730hrs. Radio Message from Division
Honouring today's victory. Expect pursuit by all possible means into the night hours.

Signed, von Manstein.

Finally, Verkhne Kumski was in German hands again, as was Sogotskot. The enemy units fled, and Battle Group Hünersdorff immediately pursued them between the two villages and onto the open plain, overrunning them easily and taking them all prisoner, *en masse*.

In the middle of this push, however, the commander was ordered to turn off east toward the familiar Hill 146.9, and on further to the Myshkova sector near the village of Vassilyevka, and to set up a bridgehead there. This objective lay at a distance of about 30km, and even without enemy contact it was clear they could not reach this location before nightfall. The unit quickly regrouped and departed.

Report
by
Commander, 6/11th Panzer Regiment
Continued ...

During the battle for Verkhne Kumski, the 17th Panzer Division was to the left, and at last in the position to take on the task of flank protection, freeing up other forces for further attacks. Everything was to be concentrated on Verkhne Kumski. The attack was deliberate and systematic, and because the individual enemy positions were known, the Stuka units were well guided as they flew in and found their targets. The grenadiers, supported by assault guns, soon broke through into the village. Having been able to watch the show from 3km away, we panzers then came in from behind, passed through our own troops in a broad front, and encountered the fleeing enemy between Verkhne Kumski and Sogotskot. As we met no resistance, and the enemy had given up group by group, I forbade further shooting. We rounded them up using just our panzers, had them put down their weapons if they had not already done so, and sent them to the rear in a closed formation where they were received by grenadiers who guarded them closely. Sogotskot, too, was taken almost without a fight.

At this moment, the radio called us together and we were briefed on our new task: to pursue, as long as the fuel lasts! The first attack objective was Hill 146.9, which we were all familiar with. As part of second battalion, I was in the lead. The day was coming to an end, and as I pushed towards Sogotskot from the south, shortly before 146.9, I ran into fire. The entire eastern horizon lit up in front of me. Panzers were also visible in the dusk. Behind us the western sky was even brighter, so much so that we must have stood out on the horizon like practice targets. The battalion was ordered to attack immediately, which would allow the enemy positions to be detected by their gunfire. As casualties grew, the commander (Dr. Bäke) broke off the battle and pulled us together behind a furrow in the earth for a new attack. In total darkness we pushed to the right, surrounding the enemy again. On the order of Major Dr.Bäke, we carried out this attack very quickly without thinking about losses, and suddenly we were right in the middle of the enemy. The battle was brutal. The shots from the enemy blinded us badly, so that their tanks only appeared as shadows moving towards us. My panzer, probably like all others that had got through, shot at an extremely high rate of fire. Enemy tanks drove past us at 10 metres; we had to be careful not to get rammed. Soon several tanks caught fire and illuminated the battlefield. Then we broke through and were once more in darkness and stillness. Behind us the steppe glowed with scattered fires and the shooting continued. Other companies kept fighting to enlarge the hole in the front, finally handing over the rest of the task to the grenadiers. Sadly, I had dead and wounded in my company, along with mechanically disabled panzers that had lost their tracks while we were overrunning the enemy anti-tank guns.

We regathered and with Oberst von Hünersdorff and Major Dr. Bäke at the furthest forward point of the advance, we moved on. The sky was clear that night and I could tell by the stars that we were moving further and further toward the east. I only knew that, cost what it would, we still had to reach the crossing point at Myshkova that night. We were told that at this bridge, we would meet up with our comrades who had broken out of the Stalingrad encirclement. This thought spurred us on all day.

This breakthrough had succeeded, and our march to the Myshkova sector continued far into the night, in completely unfamiliar terrain, and with little certainty of the enemy situation.

War Diary of 11th Panzer Regiment

2200hrs.

The march to the east takes place in moonlight, without concern for threats to the flank. Two small companies from Küper Battalion (II/114th Panzer Grenadier Regiment), which lagged somewhat further behind the remainder of the battalion, run into an enemy counterattack and remain waiting at the road intersection together with the elements that had been following them. Group Zollenkopf, which is under command of Group Hünersdorff, consists of I/114th Panzer Grenadier Regiment (Commander, Major Hauschild), I/4th Panzer Grenadier Regiment (Commander, Major Remlinger), I/76th Artillery Regiment, and anti-aircraft and anti-tank guns. It does not reach Hill 130.0 until very late. Without prospects of an immediate arrival of these units, and with the realisation that the fuel would only last as far as the expected attack position, the commander himself, who is not more than the third or fourth vehicle back from the vanguard, recklessly decides to continue on to reach the attack position. In order to retain the element of surprise, all firing is prohibited.

The original plan was to turn north at the road intersection 2km west of 157.0. But the units miss this turn-off and move on further east. Here they have to contend with terrain difficulties caused by the ravines, but at 1825hrs. they reach an intersection 2km north of Guilo Aksaiskaya, and from there they are able to turn north. Along this road are heavily occupied enemy positions, which they slip through, thanks to the calm guidance of the leader of the vanguard, Oberstleutnant Michaelis. Despite this and other challenges caused by the iced-over ravines, they surprisingly reach the bridge and cross the river. At 2200hrs, they capture the bridge intact. At the northern exit of Vassiljevka, they run into their first active enemy resistance (infantry and tanks). It is here that Michaelis is killed in action.

Battle Group Hünersdorff Radio Traffic

1750hrs. Radio Message to Division
Cannot advance on the roads in ice-covered ravine. Making new attempt by sweeping around eastwards.

1805hrs. Radio Message to Division
Zollenkopf isn't responding. Please convince him to follow as quickly as possible.

1845hrs. Radio Message to Division
On main road from south to the objective.

1922hrs. Radio Message from Division
Zollenkopf with Hauschild and Remlinger, Schulz [I/76th Artillery Regiment]. Anti-aircraft and anti-tank guns at 1800hrs. reported from Hill 130.6.

1930hrs. Radio Message to Division
Get fuel to us as quickly as possible by any available means. Convoy of armoured reconnaissance vehicles and panzer support company. Niemann ordered to report there.

1945hrs. Radio Message to Division
At bridge 6km south of target; very long delay getting through due to icy conditions.

2050hrs. Radio Message to Division
Stuck again in attempt to go through a second ravine 1km north of the previous one.

2205hrs. Radio Message to Division
Advanced through village 2km south of attack objective.

2110hrs. Radio Message to Division
Zollenkopf moving forward quickly. Elements of Küper 3km east.

2225hrs. Radio Message to Division
Zollenkopf advancing quickly. The reinforced 8th Küper, 3km east of 146.9 under heavy siege, in all-round defence position (*einigeln*).

2250hrs. Radio Message to Division

I am at attack objective, in battle with enemy tanks and infantry. Bridge in our hands.

2256hrs. Radio Message to Division

Here we only have two weak SPW companies. I'm engaged in battle with enemy tanks and infantry at the attack target. Bridge in our hands. Rapid advance by Zollenkopf urgently needed: have no fuel left.

2359hrs. Radio Message to Division

Am holding north part, which is being cleared out of enemy. Fire from tanks and mortars from outside of village has not yet been neutralised. Where is Zollenkopf?

After a night-march – with a detour of over 30km – far behind the Russian defensive positions, through several occupied enemy lines, a march over ice and snow and extremely difficult terrain, Group Hünersdorff reached the assigned objective, captured the bridge intact, and occupied the village. This march brought praise from the highest echelons; but it gave even more fuel to the hope that we could still relieve Stalingrad. Only another 48km stood between Battlegroup Hünersdorff and the surrounded and trapped army. If Generaloberst Paulus, even against the orders of the OKW – meaning Hitler – could have brought himself to decide to break out at that time, there was now a possibility of establishing contact with LVII Panzer Corps, and thereby opening the road to freedom for the majority of Paulus's divisions. The failure of the Italian army at the Donez put the overall situation of the southern front in serious jeopardy, and now a decision was urgently needed.[21]

<h3 style="text-align:center">Report
by
Commander, 6/11th Panzer Regiment
Continued ...</h3>

For me, the march to the east seemed almost endless, even surreal, enveloped as we were by total silence. The moon climbed slowly in the sky and threw our surroundings into sharp relief. The stars were clear, and the snow glowed as if lit from within. Our greatest fear was losing sight of the person in front of us.

Sometimes we struck a quick tempo, but then the vanguard would stop again and search for the assigned route. Because we crossed many of our own tracks, and the roads shown on the map were hard to make out even during the day due to the uniformity of the snow cover, the vanguard often took a wrong turn. Sometimes the leaders became stuck in a ravine that was difficult to get across. So as not to lose any time, the lead was given to the commander of whichever company was on the correct road, and the ones who had got on the wrong direction had to weave themselves back in.

Finally, Oberstleutnant Michaelis and his sharp instincts brought us to our destination. We missed the shorter route – 2km west of Hill 157.0, forking off toward Vassilyevka – which caused us to make a long detour – but then we ended up on a good road, closer to the objective, and exactly south of it. Here it would have been impossible to lose our way as a telegraph line ran along the road.

By now I was moving somewhere near the centre of the battle group. Again and again, we ran into ravines, whose ice-covered slopes glistened a strange shade of green. We were under orders not to shoot so as to avoid giving away our presence. I must admit I could never find our exact location on the map, but I trusted the vanguard and the commander. On both sides of the road, I noticed several prepared enemy positions, which to me looked very much occupied. To me this was absolutely incredible, and I found it all the more eerie when I realised the real reason for this apparent peacefulness.

Then there was a sudden halt, and we waited. My watch showed it was after 2200hrs., which meant after midnight local time. We stood panzer to panzer, having driven quite close behind one another on the road. Nearby on our right was the telegraph line, further ahead of us was a dark area, and behind it a range of mountains, crowned by what was apparently a village. Diagonally to the road, almost at my height, were well constructed panzer hull-down positions. It was very cold, and suddenly – I no longer recall how it happened – Russian soldiers were standing around our panzer, and they were armed! Out of the darkness right and left, more of them appeared. My crew and I stared through the open hatches, wondering if we were seeing things. My gunner pointed out that the Russians still had weapons on them. I shushed him and whispered in his ear, 'Quiet! They think we're Russians!' I thought at any second there would be gunfire.

Yet nothing happened. They leaned against our tracks and tried to joke around with us. Not a shot fell. What did these characters want? Didn't they notice the Wehrmacht's *Balkenkreuz*, the cross symbol of the Wehrmacht, on the sides of our vehicles? I fingered my pistol, then reached for a hand grenade from behind my seat. Just in case. My god what should we do, and how can this be taking so unbelievably long? I looked at the vehicles ahead of and behind me, and there was the same scene.

It has never been quite clear to me how we fell into this situation. There is only one likely explanation: that because we had simply rolled on into their positions in the middle of the night, making no battle sounds, the Russians thought these were their own tanks. We also arrived in a non-combat march formation, and Vassilyevka lay about 20km behind their front. At this time the Russians were still fighting against the remainder of Küper's unit at Hill 146.9, and by now may also have had to deal with Group Zollenkopf: because they were pre-occupied and it was so dark, they may not have noticed that 30 or 40 panzers had broken through their lines and were driving around somewhere in their rear area. In any case, these Russian troops had clearly not been warned against an invading panzer group.

Still, our column did not move on, and while we waited, we could easily have shot them all; but aside from the fact that we were still under a no-shoot order, we would somehow have found it repellent to shoot these curious Ivans. Instead, we had almost a quarter hour of something like fraternisation.

Suddenly, at the front of our column, the peace ended. On the hill, which was still not visible, a shot fell, soon followed by further shots and machine gun fire. We disappeared immediately into our turrets, the Russians stood in darkness on both sides of the road, and we moved slowly forward toward the village, which we could now clearly make out.

As I later learned, near the north exit of the village our vanguard panzer was destroyed by a T34 at 10 metres. The enemy tank met the same fate, but our vanguard leader, Oberstleutnant Michaelis, an admirable officer, died a hero. Over the following days we kept seeing the two tanks standing next to one another.

Still in front of the bridge, I heard loud yelling. As I looked out of the turret, a (Russian) scout car was driving backwards alongside of our column. In its turret stood a figure straight up wearing a leather vest and safety helmet. His rushed past me, his face not 3 metres away. A Russian! After overcoming the first seconds of horror, the vehicle disappeared. At the end of the column, someone shot at him as he drove off. But with no success. But surely now the Russians understood what was happening.

We entered the village, the few grenadiers dismounted, and in the light of dawn we took possession of the largest part of the rather spread-out village of Vassilyevka. But we had already captured something more important – the bridge that was still undamaged …

Thus, by midnight, the panzers of Battle Group Hünersdorff stood far forward in Vassilyevka on the Myshkova river and manned the bridgehead there. They were low on panzers, and almost out of ammunition and fuel. They had reached the objective, but would they be able to hold on to it? This was what concerned the commander. What good are tanks with no ammunition, and no fuel? The latter was the most serious concern, and the situation looked grim, as even during the march some individual panzers had come to a standstill and the crews had to be transferred to other vehicles. Moreover, there were not enough grenadier forces for the task of clearing the enemy from the village or defending against a possible enemy attack, nor was there any artillery!

Twenty kilometres back, straight south, lay 23rd Panzer Division and to the south-west was Group Zollenkopf. Both were desperately needed, but both were probably still engaged with the enemy. Would they be able fight their way to Vassilyevka before it was too late, even without the right panzer attack force? This was a matter for the division; if they were too slow in sending in supporting forces, the successes of Battle Group Hünersdorff would be squandered, and irreplaceable panzers, which were needed in further operations, would be lost.

The Russians would soon become aware of just how weak the panzer group in Vassilyevka was. In their case, it would have been a smart tactic to establish a weak ring around Vassilyevka and then go and stop the German troops north of the Aksai. But it was questionable whether there were sufficient Russian forces for this, because once the 17th Panzer Division arrived, the Russians appeared to have become splintered. Would the troops from the nearby Stalingrad encirclement be pulled out and brought here? That would mean that our operation had contributed to Paulus's break-out from the encirclement. It would all come down to timing.

The night march to Vassilyevka clearly illustrates how disadvantageous it can be to separate panzers and grenadiers. The Russians succeeded in doing this to Battle Group Hünersdorff, which almost led to a catastrophe for the battle group. The panzers in the village were almost completely on their own and were just barely holding on without fuel and ammunition; meanwhile, the grenadiers had to fight their way for 30 kilometres without panzers once more, with more problems, against an enemy who could no longer be taken by surprise. This led to casualties on both sides, which with better coordination could probably have been avoided. The assigning of blame is problematic here, but the fault in this case did not lie with the grenadiers, as can be seen in the following report:

Report
by
Commander, Battle Group Zollenkopf

At around midday of 19 Dec 1942, after two days' hard struggle, I/114th (Hauschild) broke through into the much-contested village of Verkhne Kumski. At the same time, at around 1500hrs., division orders arrived instructing Battalion Hauschild to immediately release one battery of anti-aircraft guns and one battery of artillery, which were sent to follow Group Hünersdorff. The battalion (Hauschild) was still engaged in face-to-face combat in the process of clearing the village. It was already dark, and the village was burning. To the east was a raging spectacle of firing by Group Hünersdorff in a night battle; clusters of anti-tank tracer rounds travelled back and forth across the black night skies. A truly frightening, but beautiful scene!

The I/114th had shot up all their ammunition. The companies engaged in close combat in the village had become completely mixed up with one another, and hours passed before they could regroup, bring in their vehicles, refuel, eat, and take on ammunition. At around 1900hrs., Battalion Hauschild arrived with orders to follow the tracks of the panzers made by Hünersdorff and his battalion, and after meeting up with them, to join Group Hünersdorff under its command. The staff of the 114th (Zollenkopf), along with its subordinated unit, Battalion Remlinger (I/114th *sic* and I/76th), was to follow likewise, in order that both battalions could be subordinated under Group Hünersdorff.[viii] Battalion Hauschild (I/114th) with 2/114th (Leutnant Jung) at the vanguard followed the confusing mishmash of panzer traces toward the east. The march during the dark of night was extremely difficult. The slippery slopes of the sand dunes caused the vehicles to slide and going uphill one often had to dismount and risk getting shot. At other times, wheeled vehicles were hampered by the ruts made by the panzers. Very often the columns were broken apart, and there were continual stops. Eastwards of 146.9, the battalion ran into elements of II/114th (SPWs), which had become separated from Hünersdorff and had become disoriented. Because they were continually harassed by Russians attacking from the cover of darkness,

---

viii This appears to be an error in the original. Remlinger is commander of I/4th Panzer Grenadier Regiment which was subordinate to Group Zollenkopf at this point in the operation.

they had to gather into an all-round, hedgehog defence. Driving with dimmed lights, the column of I/114th drew nearer to the Russians, who disappeared into the darkness, probably thinking the panzers would attack again.

While trying to catch up to I/114th in the darkness, the staff of 114 lost its radio station. As it was later learned, the radio station had failed due to technical problems, and this interrupted the communications to Division and Group Hünersdorff. At around midnight, the vanguard company came up against the railroad track. Thus, it was apparently too far east. After a quick re-orientation it was discovered that the panzer tracks turned to the north. The entire column then followed the tracks northwards.

After advancing a few kilometres, the vanguard company was fired on by cannons and machine gun fire. As dusk fell, a Russian field position was spotted. While the companies fell into battle positions and pulled the battery into position, the battalion was attacked by Russian fighter planes with bombs and on-board weapons. Casualties were few. The attack with 1st and 2nd /114th in front was successful; at 1000hrs., enemy resistance was defeated, and the battalion was able to regroup and mount up.

They quickly continued across a broad open plain; the terrain sloped gradually down toward the Myshkova sector. Soon several houses in Vassilyevka became visible in the morning haze. From that direction came sounds of battle. There, Group Hünersdorff was engaged in a defensive fight. No radio communication was available. The I/114th deployed in a broad front, planning to push into Vassilyevka. The commander assumed that the enemy would not be particularly strong, and that the panzers would possibly be able to neutralise the anti-tank systems they encountered. It therefore came as quite a surprise to be fired on within such a short time by artillery and anti-tank systems from the high mountains facing them. The battalion had to turn off to the right and take cover in a ravine that led to the village. Here they dismounted, with the intention of fighting on foot to the bridgehead, where Group Hünersdorff was surrounded. Shortly before nightfall, the vanguard company (2/114th) neared the southern part of the village and was fired on from individual buildings in the vicinity of the bridge.

Bringing Hauschild with him, Major Bäke left the bridgehead in an SPW and met with Hünersdorff, who briefed him on the overall situation, the enemy, and developments at the bridgehead. According to this, the most urgent issues were to reinforce the displaced panzer crews in their unaccustomed type of defensive battle, and to resupply the panzers with ammunition, which had been completely used up. Hauschild returned in the SPW, gathered his companies, circumvented the Russian-occupied southern section of the village, and swept around to the left. By crossing the ravines and fighting in constant close combat, they were able to infiltrate the village from the south-west. In our counterattacks, we recaptured some of the buildings and strengthened defences. On the same road came munitions and some fuel for the panzers. With this, two of the most urgent tasks had been accomplished. The battle strength of the companies had shrunk to about 50 per cent during the battles of recent days. Unfortunately, Leutnant Jung, the courageous and highly respected commander of 2nd Company, was fatally wounded, and Leutnant Kelletat, Commander of 3/114th, fell in battle. Thus, in recent days, I/114th alone suffered three irretrievable losses. A night attack was declined because the incoming battalion was unfamiliar with the terrain, the front was fully closed, and neither our heavy weapons nor the tanks or artillery could offer even the slightest support. An attack toward the north-west, whose intent was to first clear the village of enemy and then capture the hills north of the village, was postponed to the next day.

Wehrmacht Report of 20 December 1942

(Excerpt)

Between the Volga and Don, German panzer divisions, attacking a tough enemy defence, and in cooperation with Romanian troops, captured an important river sector.

As is clearly shown in following two documents, it was becoming urgent that the surrounded Sixth Army come to a decision:[22]

Letter from von Manstein to Army Chief-of-Staff

By hand of officers only	3 Copies
Secret material for command headquarters	3 Copies
Matter for high-level commanders	19 Dec. 1435hrs.

Secret material for high level command, by the hand of officers only

To: Chief-of-Staff of the Army
for immediate submission to the Führer

The situation at Army Group Don, due to developments at Army Group B and the cutting off of further forces, has developed to the point that an extraction of Sixth Army cannot be considered for the foreseeable future.

The supply, and thereby the maintenance of the army in the fortress area by air, has proven impossible due to reasons of available resources as well as weather, as has been demonstrated over the four weeks since the encirclement. LVII Panzer Corps obviously cannot even establish contact with Sixth Army by land, let alone preserve it. I now believe the final possibility is for the army to break out of the encirclement from the south-west, by which means at least the majority of the soldiers and the elements of the army that are still mobile can be preserved.

The break-out, whose first goal is to establish contact with the LVII Panzer Corps, can only be accomplished somewhere at the Yerik Myshkova, by a gradual pushing of the army toward the south-west, which will take place through combat, in the manner that will expand the fortress area, vacating one section at a time in the north, while gradually pushing toward the south-west.

During this operation, it will be necessary to use sufficient pursuit and fighter planes to furnish supplies by air.

Because there is already apparent enemy pressure toward the north flank of the Fourth Romanian Army, forces from the Caucasus front must be brought here quickly, by any and all means, to provide security for the deep right flank of LVII Panzer Corps, to enable it to carry out its task.

In case of any further delay, it is foreseeable that LVII Panzer Corps will come to a standstill at or north of the Myshkova, or become tied up through attacks at its right flank. With this, the combined effects of the attacks from within and outside will be overtaken by events. Before deploying, Sixth Army will need several days to regroup and refuel.

Food supplies inside the ring area sufficient through 22 Dec. Already great weakening of the soldiers (for last 14 days, only 200 g of bread). Majority of the horses, according to statement from the army, have already been side-lined due to exhaustion or eaten.

The Commander in Chief of Army Group Don
signed v. Manstein, Generalfeldmarschall
signed Schulz
Ia No. 0368/42 Secret Top Priority Matter [Geh.Kdos.Chefsache]

Letter from v. Manstein for Sixth Army and Fourth Panzer Army

Secret Command Document	5 Copies
Top Priority	4 Copies

Officers only   19 Dec. 1800hrs.
Secret Command Document – for officers only

For Commanders
Sixth Army
Fourth Panzer Army

1. Fourth Panzer Army has defeated the enemy in the area of Verkhne Kumski with
    LVII Panzer Corps and has reached the Myshkova sector at Nish Kimski.[23] [24]
    Attacks against strong enemy groups in area of Kamenka and north have
    begun. Hard fighting still expected.

    Situation at Chir front does not allow advance of forces west of the Don
toward Kalach. Chirskaya in enemy hands.

2. Sixth Army is to deploy for the *Wintergewitter* (*Winter Thunderstorm*) attack as
    soon as possible.[25] Thereby it is expected that, if necessary, the link-up with
    LVII Panzer Corps in order to get the convoy through will be done by way
    of the Donskaya Zaritza.

3. The development of the situation could force the mission outlined in paragraph
    2. to be extended, so that when the army breaks out, it will link up with
    LVII Panzer Corps on the Myshkova. Code word *Donnerschlag* (*Thunderclap*).
    It is a matter of getting panzers to LVII Panzer Corps so that they can get
    the convoy through under the cover of the flank at the lower Karpovka, and
    then lead the army toward the Myshkova as it leaves the fortress area.

    Donnerschlag must at all costs operate directly in conjunction with *Wintergewitter*.
Support by air will essentially have to be carried out on a continuous basis
without a great deal of preparation. It is important to hold Pitomnik airfield for
as long as possible.

    All movable weapons and artillery are to be brought out, especially all guns
that are required for battle, and are to be loaded, as are the heavy and hard-to-
replace weapons and equipment. These are to be assembled in the south-west
area in ample time.

4. Advance preparations must be made as in Paragraph 3. Do not deploy until
    ordered with the command, *Donnerschlag*.

5. Attack day and time will be reported to Number 2.

    Commander in Chief, Army Group Don
    Ia No. 0369/42 Secret High Priority Document dtd. 19 Dec 1942

                                signed v. Manstein, Generalfeldmarschall

5 copies	3. Q Branch
1. Signal office (original)	4. War Diary
2. Air Fleet 4	5. Draft

20 December 1942
LVII Panzer Corps and the Push
to the Myshkova
Map 14

War Diary of 11th Panzer Regiment

Vassilyevka, 20 Dec 1942

0600hrs.

The slowly developing enemy opposition grows stronger over the course of the night. Our own weak forces – only 21 panzers without fuel and two weak SPW companies – are not enough to expand the bridgehead to the extent that a further advance is possible. Commander therefore orders them to take a position of all-round defence on the north bank of the river. Amid constantly growing enemy pressure, with continual heavy bombardment by infantry, artillery, and anti-tank guns and mortars, we fend off several enemy attacks and can hold the bridgehead, hoping for relief from Group Zollenkopf by the following day.

0900hrs.

At 0430hrs., we fend off the first strong advance by enemy infantry from the north-west. But the commander is aware that we can expect stronger attacks in the course of the 20th. Yesterday evening via radio message, the commander ordered the commander of the staff company of II/11th Panzer Regiment, who is in charge of the pooled repair service, to consolidate the repaired panzers in Salivski into one company and form a convoy for transporting fuel and munitions forward. But the company was co-opted by Division and pulled forward to support Group Zollenkopf. The attack by Group Zollenkopf is visible off in the distance, but as yet they have gained no further ground. From constant firing of tanks and anti-tank guns, more panzers are disabled. The dismounted crews are being deployed as infantry to reinforce the grenadiers.

Battle Group Hünersdorff Radio Traffic

0450hrs. Radio Message to Division
Constant bombardment from tanks and mortars. Advance of enemy infantry from the north-west is halted. Attack objective north of the river is held. Heavy enemy attacks expected over the course of the 20th. Still have 21 panzers without fuel.

0620hrs. Radio Message to Division
Why is the consolidated Niemann Company still being held up?

Still have 18 vehicles without fuel. Urgently request relief.

0725hrs. Radio Message to Division
Constant bombardment from heavy mortars and tanks. Repeated advances by small units were fended off. Counterattack not possible, as no fuel. Two Küper companies are too weak to expand bridgehead.

0735hrs. Radio Message to Division
Request air support against enemy on hills hard north of the bridgehead. Inform as to appointed time of attack.

1235hrs. Radio Message from Division

Proposed mission for 21 Dec: Turn off to the north. Division order to follow.

Division Battle Staff. Klykovo

1325hrs. Radio Message from Division
To Oberst v. Hünersdorff, to you, and to all panzer gunners and panzer grenadiers, my full recognition and thanks for your guts and fortitude. General Raus.

By morning the vanguard of the long wished-for Battle Group Zollenkopf was visible to the south, although one had to realise that between the northern, higher hills and the southern bank of the Myshkova there was an elevation difference of about 30 metres. With this, Battle Group Hünersdorff, which was encircled in the northern part of Vassilyevka, could see as far as 5km into the southern terrain, which was lower and gradually sloped up to the horizon. What could be seen coming from the area of Battle Group Zollenkopf were some individual impacts from their artillery along the southern horizon. But these might also have been the artillery fire from 23rd Panzer Division, which was also slowly advancing.

Nevertheless, watching our battle groups as they came near, knowing relief was on its way, was of great reassurance. The enemy attacked the villages almost without pause, but because his attacks were so unsystematic, they were fiercely fought off.

Except for the bridge ramp, however, the entire southern bank of the river, along with the houses there that belonged to the village, were now transferred into Russian hands. The ammunition was being used up quickly, including machine gun ammunition. Something had to happen soon.

War Diary of 11th Panzer Regiment

1600hrs.

The enemy is constantly being reinforced, but still only attacks some of the time, and with small units. Contact with Zollenkopf is not yet established. Zollenkopf is instructed by radio message to immediately capture several houses on the southern bank near the bridge in order to enable two grenadier companies and scout vehicles to move past them into the bridgehead. As to the orders from Division that on the 21st we turn off to the north, the commander finds this very problematic, as the panzer regiment and SPW battalion would have to be re-assembled again, and no one will be able to count on the communications to the rear. At 1530hrs., the enemy breaks through from the north-west. Throwing him out on our own is no longer a possibility.

1900hrs.

At 1645hrs. the first of the company commanders from I/114th Panzer Grenadier Regiment arrives, but with only a few people. By 1900hrs, only two platoons of I/114th (Battalion Hauschild) are at the bridgehead. Impossible to get scout vehicles through the southern front, but the plan is to do so during the night. Without this, the breach to the north-west of the bridgehead cannot yet be rectified. At dawn, once all of Hauschild has arrived, commander intends to lead an attack out and to the west of the bridgehead onto the hill north-west of Vassilyevka, in order then to deploy further out from there.

Due to lack of water, noticeable exhaustion among the crews at the bridgehead, with suffering especially among the wounded. Since yesterday at midday, at total of 25 panzers are side-lined, some for mechanical problems, but most due to shelling. First Battalion has only seven deployable panzers.

Battle Group Hünersdorff Radio Traffic

1315hrs. Radio Message to Division

Enemy constantly reinforced but has not attempted renewed attack. Breakthrough by two companies on SPWs not possible so far due to heavy defence. Zollenkopf instructed to capture several buildings near the bridge in order to enable the SPWs to enter.

1415hrs. Radio Message to Division

Am stopping now as before, in face of enemy forays and heavy bombardment. Not counting on arrival of Hauschild before 1700hrs.

For possible continuation of action, request addition of strong grenadier force to prevent miserable situations such as this one today, as the troops are very worn down.

1600hrs. Radio Message to Division

Day's report: after a short battle, breakthrough in enemy defence line south-west of 146.9. With careful advance, hampered only by terrain difficulties, the enemy was completely surprised, and the bridgehead was taken after a short battle. Due to shortage of resources and fuel, the bridgehead at the north bank had to be kept very small.[26] All day and night, the enemy attacked continuously, and due to the immobility of our vehicles, we incurred heavy losses. Enemy broke through at 1530hrs. from the north-west and could only be thrown back again with help from Hauschild.

Launching battle early morning is questionable, as panzers and Küper must first be re-grouped, and the fuel and munitions have not yet arrived.

1615hrs. Radio Message from Division

Zollenkopf instructed to reach Vassilyevka as quickly as possible. Lead element of 6th Reconnaissance Battalion, 1505hrs. passed Hill 146.9.

1645hrs. Radio Message to Division

One company commander from Hauschild arrived. Mop-up scheduled.

1840hrs. Radio Message to Division

Enemy attack from north and west, not carried out further as yet. Breakthrough not yet rectified, as only two platoons from Hauschild are at the bridgehead. During the night two companies are to be brought in on SPWs through the weak enemy-held area into the bridgehead area. At dawn, the Hauschild attack from out of the bridgehead and to the west on the high hills to the north, Remlinger on enemy-owned south sector with support of newly provided panzers. After establishing communications, expand bridgehead, organise the units at the bridgehead, reload ammunition and fuel. Only then is renewed action possible. For radio equipment, necessary fuel is to be brought forward during the night on SPWs.

At bridgehead considerable casualties due to heavy shelling. Troops very strained because of no quiet, no warm food, and no shelter.

? hrs. Radio Message to Division

Casualties at bridgehead:

11th Panzer Regiment: Deaths: Oberstleutnant Michaelis, 7 NCOs and soldiers; wounded: Assistenzarzt Dr. Schmidt, 16 NCOs and soldiers.

114th Panzer Grenadier Regiment: deaths: Oberstleutnant Jäger, 24 NCOs and soldiers; wounded: Oberstleutnant Jung, 36 NCOs and soldiers.

57th Pioneer Battalion: deaths: 3 NCOs and soldiers; wounded: 7 NCOs and soldiers.

Disabled vehicles: 25 panzers, some mechanical, some from shelling, 5 SPWs.

Successes: two T34s, one Christie, four 4.7 anti-tank systems, three 7.62 anti-tank systems, 165 prisoners taken, approx. 150 kills, numerous infantry weapons and anti-tank rifles.

1900hrs. Radio Message from I Battalion/11th Panzer Regiment

Panzer count: 0/4/2/0/1[27]

Toward the end of the day there was even a scouting foray with Group Zollenkopf. Still we did not push back the enemy south of the sector, who may have been weak, but remained tenacious. The division's situation toward evening was as follows: Battle Group Hünersdorff without fuel and ammunition in an all-round defensive position in the north section of the village, but still occupying the bridge; with them were elements of the Küper Battalion (II/114th Panzer Grenadier Regiment) on the southern riverbank, almost without contact with the panzers; Group Zollenkopf with the Hauschild Battalion (I/114th Panzer Grenadier Regiment). Behind Zollenkopf, on the march toward Vassilyevka, were I/4th Panzer Grenadier Regiment (Remlinger) and Group Quentin (mainly the 6th Reconnaissance Battalion), followed by the rest of Group Unrein with II/4th Panzer Grenadier Regiment. Elements of the 23rd Panzer Division on the right side of the division, toward Birsovoi, which Hünersdorff had already crossed during the night of the 19th. To the left of the division, the 17th pushed toward Gromoslavka, without having reached the Myshkova sector to this point.

With this came the urgent task of clearing out the southern riverbank and the nearby outskirts of Vassilyevka. Here the enemy were few in number but were tough fighters with a well-constructed system of positions inside the buildings. Both these enemy units and those on the northern riverbank, which stood at a higher elevation, had so far been able to prevent any sizeable flow of munitions, fuel, and soldiers in SPWs into the bridgehead. From the hill to the north, on both sides of the village, the Russians had a good view the southern bank and dominated it, mainly with their anti-tank guns. The terrain was almost bare and without cover, and our own artillery could not find effective positions.

The 21st of December promised to be a day of battle. It was clear to us that once the Russians realised the long-term consequences of our attack on Vassilyevka, they too would bring in new forces. After all, the fortunes of the entire German front from Aksai to the Myshkova sector now turned on the strength of the first breakthrough by Battle Group Hünersdorff. The next push by the Germans would be from this village in the direction of Stalingrad. For the Russians everything depended on their putting a stop to this attack with all their might, and ultimately safeguarding the encirclement around Stalingrad. This was a crucial moment, but not just for the Sixth Army – should a break-out succeed at this time, the Russians would have a dilemma on their hands.

This was the last chance for Generaloberst Paulus to save his army, and the decision had to be made immediately. The situation at the southern front left doubts as to whether Army Group Don could still fuel and otherwise sustain both the front at the Chir river and the advance by LVII Panzer Corps south of the Don. Back on 18 December, during the first assault, the enemy had broken through the Italian Army at the mid-Don, at the junction of Army Group B and Army Group Don. Now a large number of enemy mechanised and tank corps were on the move toward the Donez and the Tatzinskaya and Morosovskaya bases, which were vital for the German air support to Stalingrad. At that moment there was nothing to stop them. If the Russians could not be brought to a halt before they reached Rostov, there was the danger of a crisis even worse than Stalingrad, in which the entire Army Group Don and Army Group A, now fighting in the Caucasus, would also be surrounded. But what resources were available to Army Group B and Army Group Don at this point? As of 20 December, practically nothing. The OKW had promised to bring in the 7th Panzer Division, due to arrive from France, plus some individual Luftwaffe field divisions. But the minor combat power of a Luftwaffe field division would be irrelevant, and in any case, none of these forces would be able to arrive in time to save the situation.

If Generaloberst Paulus did not immediately decide to break out of the encirclement, then there would have to be a regrouping within Army Group Don in order to secure their open left flank, which extended hundreds of kilometres. The necessary divisions, however, could be pulled from only from the Chir front and the LVII Panzer Corps, which was fighting south of the Don. For the most part, all other fronts consisted of allied divisions, which were either unreliable and on the verge of disintegrating, or so deeply engaged in defensive battles that pulling them out would lead to new catastrophes.

Ultimately this all added up to a 'temporary' abandonment of the plan to liberate Stalingrad, and along with it – as was no doubt clear to every commander – was a death sentence for the encircled Sixth Army.

If General Paulus would not make an immediate decision to break out, and would not shoulder this risk himself, only a miracle could save him. And it was a risk, as he might not have succeeded in pushing on through until the German troops met up with the LVII Panzer Corps, be it in the direction of the Don or to the south-west. And out in the open steppe, torn loose from his solid positions, his troops might have met the same fate.

Wehrmacht Report of 21 December 1942

[Excerpt]

In the Volga-Don region, heavy fighting continues. In fierce tank and infantry battles, the Soviets again suffered extremely high losses in men and materiel.

21 December 1942
Holding the Bridgehead at Vassilyevka

War Diary of 11th Panzer Regiment

Vassilyevka, 21 Dec 1942

0600hrs.

With all ammunition depleted, the situation at the bridgehead has become more and more critical overnight. The enemy attacks again and again, using a concentric pattern, and can only be fended off through close combat. At 0000hrs. and for some time after, the Russians were no more than 15m from the Hünersdorff command post, the heart of the bridgehead. The commander called for the soldiers, who were physically and mentally exhausted, to counterattack and to continue to stand fast. Fuel has become so scarce that the radio traffic must be limited, as there is no way to recharge the dying batteries. The troops are at the end of their strength due to the constant fighting, lack of rest, lack of warm food, water, and shelter, all of which is felt more harshly in the increasingly cold temperatures.

In the early morning hours, just two Hauschild companies are at the bridgehead, which are just enough to hold off any enemy breakthrough. The arrival of SPW companies proves to be just as impossible as before. Despite all orders, under these conditions any plans for further deployment are unthinkable, as are any adjustments to the bridgehead. The shelling from weapons of all sorts, which now include artillery, Stalin's organs, and fighter planes, greatly increases our casualties. Our weapons can hardly compete.

Battle Group Hünersdorff Radio Traffic

0612hrs. Radio Message from Division

Attack by Zollenkopf begins 0530hrs. Continued advance to ordered objective after clearing of the area around the bridgehead.

0850hrs. Radio Message to Division
    Vanguard of attack Remlinger south-east perimeter of Kaptinka. Hauschild south-west perimeter Vassilyevka.

0945hrs. Radio Message to Division
    Vanguard of Zollenkopf already turned in at village perimeter.

1000hrs. Message to Division

The attack by Group Zollenkopf which began at 0530hrs. has succeeded. At 0900hrs. the battalion on the right, I/4th (Remlinger), broke through into the south-western village perimeter of Kaptinka. Hauschild stayed on the left and established contact with the south.

1130hrs. Radio Message from Division
    After arrival of necessary reinforcements, seizing hills north of Vassilyevka, security measures at Hill 124.05km east of Vassilyevka and Hill 109.5, 4½km north-east of Vassilyevka. Reconnaissance toward east, north, and west. Establish communication with Boineburg [23rd Panzer Division] direction Gnilo-Aksaiskaya.

1345hrs. Radio Message to Division

Requesting Zollenkopf's arrival here with me soon, otherwise I cannot move, and Zollenkopf must take command of elements not deployed at bridgehead.

1430hrs. Radio Message to Division

Zollenkopf just arrived here. Remlinger and Hauschild still in fight over enemy ground bunker positions north of the village. Near the north-east flank, enemy tanks and infantry on the attack, panzer support deployed against them. Whether or not bunker positions can still be taken before darkness, appears doubtful.

Intent: hold bridgehead.

The withdrawal of panzers as close shock force not possible at the moment, as infantry are not certain to hold out without panzers behind them. At the bridgehead, deployed elements of Küper are so worn down that their use as attack troops not possible at this time.

After a very tense night, Group Zollenkopf attacked successfully, warding off the most dangerous threat to Battle Group Hünersdorff. Because of the order placing Zollenkopf under von Hünersdorff, the rare situation arose in which commander of a surrounded unit became the commander of the unit sent to relieve him at Vassilyevka. The relationship may have been difficult prior to the development of this situation at Vassilyevka (radio message of 19 Dec 1942, 1450hrs). That the relationship proved untenable is evident in the radio message of 21 Dec (1345hrs.)

The division – under pressure from the corps – repeatedly attempted to get the advance underway in order to meet up with the surrounded troops as close to Stalingrad as possible. This resolve, a valid one in and of itself, flew in the face of the actual reality: at that point Battle Group Hünersdorff was no longer battle-worthy.

The order for the continued advance was announced by the division on 20 Dec. But according to a radio message (1235hrs.), it appears to have already reached the hands of Oberst von Hünersdorff ahead of time.

As the War Diary of the 11th Panzer Regiment states, and as the division itself came to realise, even considering the shortage of time this order had been scheduled prematurely.

War Diary of 11th Panzer Regiment

1500hrs.

Our continued attack against the hills to the north-west, north, and north-east of the bridgehead proves to be very difficult, as the enemy is very strong and sits in ground bunkers. The enemy deploys new forces, including tanks, against the north-east corner of the bridgehead, which presents some threat to our panzers. Clearing the hills is no longer successful. The attack of the panzer grenadiers must be broken off at nightfall. This means that the bridge position remains under further direct shelling. When Zollenkopf arrives, commander reports that the use of the panzer as close attack force for the time is not possible, as the panzer grenadiers, without the panzers behind them would certainly not hold out. The elements of the SPW battalion deployed in the bridgehead are so exhausted that using them as attack troops is not possible.

2100hrs.

Commander is ordered to division battle command post for conference on situation and intent.

Battle Group Hünersdorff Radio Traffic

1630hrs. Radio message to Division

Hill 110.4 in our hands. Bunker position north of the hill and at north-west perimeter of the village of Vassilyevka could not be taken. Artillery shelling from north and north-west direction. Cannon, mortar, and machine gun fire from defensive nests in local area. We are holding Vassilyevka and 110.4.

1650hrs. Radio Message to Division

Decrease in artillery support not tenable. Formation of mobile panzer spearhead initially not possible, as tanks must remain as backup for infantry and are allocated to positions.

A renewed assembly will only be possible after removal of enemy bunker positions.

A Summary
by
Commander, 6/11th Panzer Regiment

The first two days were the most difficult for us in Vassilyevka. While the other parts of the division slowly fought their way closer to this sector, we were positioned forward, occupying the only useable bridge leading to Stalingrad, having to hold out against the extremely hard Russian counterattacks. Almost all hours, day or night, the Russians, concentrated or individually, deployed their weapons. Always pressed into a tight area, we no longer exited our vehicles. The few grenadiers among us positioned themselves under our panzers, or dug in near to us, bursting forth only for occasional counterattacks under our fire support. Because we were without fuel, we could not move. Each panzer had his sector, but a close command was no longer possible, and one saw only his sector, his grenadiers, and his crew. The almost constant fire from artillery and the Stalin's organs, which came in hurricane-like surges proclaiming new attacks, was most aggravating and caused the most casualties. This caused the losses of panzer after panzer, and among the casualties was one of my best platoon leaders, Feldwebel Reusch. Our deepest concern was for the wounded. We no longer had anywhere to lay them out, as the last houses had caught fire or sunk into ruins. Added to this was the lack of water, and the bitter outside cold.

The first two days we were completely cut off from supplies and had no artillery of our own with which we could have defeated the enemy. We did have Stukas – JU88s (*sic*) – which brought occasional, noticeable relief, and which grew more effective each day. From a low altitude they dropped bombs only a few metres in front of us, and right into the Russian attack forces. While we also took serious casualties, soon the outskirts of the village were strewn with Russian dead as a result of the persistent [German] air attacks.

While on the way to see the regimental commander, Oberst von Hünersdorff, who had his command post in a hole under his panzer, I was shot as well. A bullet lodged between my ribs. It was all a miracle, as the shot, which itself was very painful, was impeded by the thickness of winter clothing, my tobacco pipe, and my cigarette case, which it penetrated, but ended up causing no harm. The impact knocked me down. Fellow soldiers pulled me under a panzer, and the doctor removed shot right there on the spot. I assume it was not a targeted shot, but instead something that came from far off, as otherwise the padding would not have helped. At least this way I could still stay with my company.

Group Zollenkopf's attack brought significant relief as well as ammunition and fuel. Our artillery became all the stronger in its defensive fighting and on the 22nd, with the use of flame throwers, the grenadiers cleared out the last pockets of resistance.

Report on events of 21 December
by Oberst Zollenkopf,
Commander, 114th Panzer Grenadier Regiment

During the night Remlinger's battalion was also affected. In order to expand the bridgehead toward the right, the commander of the 114th engaged the battalion in an attack on the southern part of the village, after whose capture the follow-on mission would be to turn off toward the right through the Myshkova trough and capture Kaptinka.

Both battalions began their attack at 0530hrs., now effectively supported by heavy weapons, smoke mortars, and artillery. Despite our low battle strength and great fatigue from constant overexertion, the attack went forward. Close to midday, the I/4th succeeded in breaking into Kaptinka, and the I/114th cleared out the west part of the village. The enemy constantly received reinforcements and was in position on the hill north of the village in dug-in bunkers. So, the I/114th and the I/4th were not able to capture these hills, which still ruled over the southern part of the village and the bridge. The battalion set up their defence of Kaptinka and the northern perimeter of Vassilyevka. The supply route had been fought open, and the bridgehead was expanded and strengthened. After finishing this task, the staff of Zollenkopf began modifying positions in the village, in which almost the entire division was now assembled in a defensive front.

The fronts were now solidified, and neither the Russians nor the 6th Panzer Division were able to free up forces for another thrust.

As part of the LVII Panzer Corps, the division had gained over 100 kilometres, and now there were still 48 kilometres between the furthest forward units and the Stalingrad encirclement. They had fought their way through three quarters of the entire distance, and it was unclear to everyone as to why the other army was not coming to meet them. Surely two hundred thousand soldiers ought to be able to fight their way across 50 kilometres. That day more than enough rumours swirled around us. Someone claimed to know for certain that the Sixth Army had already deployed, while someone else claimed to have already spoken with someone from Stalingrad who was part of the advance guard from the main body of the army, which had already made contact with the relief troops at some neighbouring sector or another. Still others spoke of a connecting passage across the steppe, where materiel was already rolling in toward the Sixth Army.

The only bit of genuine news was that the Fourth Panzer Army at Kotelnikovo was preparing a large depot area to enable the immediate transport of urgently needed materiel on a soon-to-be-won corridor to Stalingrad.

But General Paulus had not yet launched the break-out. He had likely received the break-out order from his direct superior, Generalfeldmarschall Manstein, commander in chief of Army Group Don. But at the same moment, Hitler forbade any break-out that would involve giving up ground that had already been captured. To bring both demands into compliance would have been impossible, not just for Paulus, but for any other army commander as well. Moreover, Generaloberst Paulus harboured doubts as to whether it was at all possible, given his scant fuel and ammunition, to manage to break out and advance as far as the relief army. Given that he would have been in defiance of Hitler's order, and given the lack of the necessary materiel, it is unclear as to whether Paulus would have taken it upon himself to risk a break-out. But such question marks and moral dilemmas remain beyond the scope of this book.[28]

It was primarily left to the Army Group Don to create a connecting corridor to the encirclement, and without help from those inside the encirclement. Its forces were too weak, and at that point in time and due to the overall situation, the task still proved to be impossible.

On the evening of 21 December, the Russians broke through the Italian Army at the Don with their advance guard and were close to the important Donez bridge at Kamensk-Shakhtinsky. At Millerovo, farther north, a small German contingent that had already been surrounded barely held on. What took place in the area between the Donez and Morosovskaya was not quite clear, but there was no longer a continuous defensive front there. At the lower and middle Chir was the Army Detachment Hollidt, to the left, with a completely open left flank; then came remnants of the Third Romanian Army with some stand-in units and some worn-down air force field divisions, forming a front that could be quickly penetrated by any reasonably strong Russian foray. Attached to this, with its right flank at the Don in the region of the mouth of the Chir, was the XLVIII Panzer Corps, whose mission it had once been to operate in conjunction with LVII Panzer Corps in clearing the route to

Stalingrad. Due to the constant defensive battles toward the north and the withdrawal of the divisions that had been designated for the task, this never took place.

In a very short time, the Russians had covered far more than the half the route to the Asov Sea from their starting point on the Don in front of the Italian Army. In the most dangerous area between Voroshilovgrad on the Donez and Morosovskaya at the large bend in the Don River, the Russians had no strong enemy forces in front of them. It would not take more than a few days for a huge catastrophe to develop. The only parts of Army Group Don with combat strength, the XLVIII and the LVII Panzer Corps, lay 200km further to the east on their way to relieve Stalingrad. The Italian Army and the majority of the Third Romanian Army had disappeared from the battlefield. Now the two German panzer corps were in danger of being surrounded like the Sixth Army, and further, once the Russians reached Rostov, Army Group A would have no route of retreat.

22 December 1942
Repulsing All Attacks

War Diary of 11th Panzer Regiment

0635hrs.

The night passed with the usual enemy forays, but with help from the two panzer grenadier battalions and support from the artillery deployed outside of the bridgehead, we were able to defeat them more easily than on the previous days.

Shortly after 0600hrs., the enemy attacked from the north-east with a regiment-size force, and from the south-east with about 15 tanks. The II/11th Panzer Regiment fended off the tank attack, hit four of their tanks, and pursued the enemy, who then turned away and escaped.[29]

Battle Group Hünersdorff Radio Traffic

0635hrs. Radio Message to Division

Enemy attacks with strength of an infantry regiment from the north-east, from the south-east with tanks, so far 12 sighted. Tank attack defeated, four destroyed, pursuit!

0910hrs. Radio Message to Division

Continued enemy attacks from north-east, and tanks appear. Probably the ones that were previously fought in the south-east. To the south-east, the enemy attack is halted for now. Hauschild and Remlinger are holding their positions. Kreis [II/4th Panzer Grenadier Regiment] moves into security position toward the east and south. Enemy apparently strongest in the south-east.

0915hrs. Radio Message to Division

Luftwaffe support requested against the enemy from north-east and south-east.

0920hrs. Radio Message from Division

By order of corps headquarters (*Generalkommando*), attack immediately toward the north-east by way of Farm 1 (location code) to reach ordered march objective.

A comparison of the two bridgeheads, Salivski vs. Vassilyevka, might be useful here. On the Aksai, one reinforced battalion (Remlinger) was sufficient for defence, but both grenadier regiments were deployed there, so that the division was unable to deploy a combat-ready shock troop for a sustained attack. In Salivski the regiment had grown much stronger and had been able to ward off the enemy, thanks mostly to the panzers that had been forward deployed in Verkhne Kumski. This meant that the enemy, with his essentially weaker forces, would have to concentrate them fully on Salivski. Nevertheless, it was a rather weak 6th Panzer Division that now stood face to face with a very strong enemy, which had been reinforced by the addition of reserves and units pulled from the Stalingrad encirclement.

Therefore, when Division issued the order (0920hrs.) to continue advancing immediately, this could only have happened under strict instructions from a higher-level command.

War Diary of 11th Panzer Regiment

1000hrs.

Enemy continues to attack from the north-east, now with tanks as well, probably some that had already been defeated in the south-east. The attack from the north-east is successfully defeated. Because the commander assumes that the enemy is strongest in the south-east and is preparing for a new attack, the newly arrived II/4th Panzer Grenadier Regiment (Kreis) is deployed south of the Myshkova, with its front facing east, south-east, and south. Luftwaffe support requested for enemy attacks, which increase constantly. These pose a threat to the front, as our artillery and the rocket battalions assigned to them meanwhile have no visibility from behind the mountains. To hold the front, extreme effort and commitment of all elements will be needed. Despite this, the corps nevertheless orders an attack from the bridgehead toward Verkhne Zarizinski, the last stretch of ground before reaching Stalingrad. The commander reports the impossibility of further deployment.

Battle Group Hünersdorff Radio Traffic

1005hrs. Radio Message to Division

Defending from heavy enemy attack from north-east and south-east. Holding out only with greatest exertion. Everything deployed. No forces available for ordered attack. Corps staff can be personally assured of this.

1220hrs. Radio Message to Division

Very large infantry columns advancing from north-west to Vassilyevka. Luftwaffe support requested. Beginning 1215hrs., 5km north-west of Vassilyevka.

1255hrs. Radio Message to Division

Heydebreck [23rd Panzer Division] 1146hrs. attacked at Birsovoi. Enemy attack warded off.

1335hrs. Radio Message to Division

Situation unchanged. Attack against Heydebreck outside of Birsovoi halted for now.

Brisk enemy air activity.

On 22 December the Russians deployed a ground attack aviation unit which came on stronger than on previous days, and whose rocket fire made life especially miserable. Yet here too, the Russians showed their weaknesses in terms of leadership: they deployed all of their weapons with great force, but seldom managed to organise a coordinated, combined arms attack. What happened repeatedly was that they first allowed their infantry to bear down, and then after it took its beating, set the tanks on attack, and finally without any coordinated action, let loose with the artillery. Or all of the above in a different order. They deployed their troops as they became available without waiting until everything could move together in a well-settled, simultaneous, meaningful attack.

War Diary of 11th Panzer Regiment

1400hrs.

Reconnaissance reports very large infantry columns at 1212hrs. from the north-west toward Vassilyevka. Beginning at 1215hrs., 5km north-west of the village. Combat air units deployed against them to good effect. With its attack on Birsovoi, the 23rd Panzer Division provides relief against enemy coming in from south-east, but this does not lead to capture of the village. Enemy air activity growing heavier.

1700hrs.

The enemy has halted his attacks for the time being and has dug in at his presently occupied lines.

1900hrs.

The commander reports intent for 23 December: 0500hrs.: attack by Hauschild Battalion to capture the north-west hill. At 0700hrs., attack by Remlinger Battalion for recapture of Hill 110.4. According to situation, regroup for advance northward.

Battle Group Hünersdorff Radio Traffic

1630hrs. Radio Message to Division

Enemy dug in at his present line, south-west, east, and north-east. In the north-eastern part of Kaptinka, enemy movements. Enemy pressure has decreased.

1900hrs. Radio Message to Division

Intent, 23 Dec: at 0500hrs., attack by Hauschild to capture hill (north-western hill). At 0700hrs., attack by Remlinger to capture 110.4. Then according to the situation, regroup for advance northward.

At 0700hrs., Luftwaffe support, especially fighters, at mid-to-north-east Kaptinka and northern perimeter 110.4.

Thanks to the successful deployment of the Luftwaffe, the addition of a fourth grenadier battalion from the division, the attack by the 23rd Panzer Division on Birsovoi and the formation of a second bridgehead at Gromoslavka by the 17th Panzer Division, the enemy pressure on Vassilyevka over the course of 22 December decreased. With this we came closer to being able to advance further in the foreseeable future, or more specifically, to put together a battle group from the defensive front.

Events of recent days showed once more how just one unit that has penetrated deeply into the enemy's territory can enable a neighbouring unit to advance, just by holding on and tying up a number of enemy forces (see also the advance by Battle Group Hünersdorff on Verkhne Kumski).

The situation of the overall Army Group Don, however, had become more serious. The Russians and their vanguard were positioned between Voroshilovgrad and Forchstadt close to the Donez; Tatzinskaya, the important air supply base for Stalingrad, was about to fall. Army Detachment Hollidt abandoned the upper Chir and turned back to the west, now completely deserted by the remnants of the Third Romanian Army that had been assigned under them. Because of the absence of the Romanians, the XLVIII Panzer Corps, at the lower Chir and its mouth into the Don, was now almost completely without contact with Hollidt.

On orders from Army Group Don, the XLVIII Panzer Corps now had to give up its strongest force, the 11th Panzer Division, so that it could move to Morosovskaya to prevent the capture of Tatzinskaya. At the same time, however, it was very doubtful whether the corps could still hold on at its former position at all.

If Feldmarschall v. Manstein, as commander in chief of Army Group Don, despite Fourth Panzer Army's situation south of the Don, still allowed it to continue attacking in the direction of Stalingrad, and even demanded increased activity, this only shows how very much he strove toward a liberating of Stalingrad, and still hoped that Generaloberst Paulus would decide to break out of the encirclement. The hour was near, however – although in the meantime the Sixth Army made no visible effort to cooperate with the relief army – when forces would have to be pulled out in order to prevent a breach by the Russians at the Sea of Asov. Army Group Don could no longer offer to rescue the Sixth Army without placing one million German soldiers at risk.

Wehrmacht Report of 23 December 1942

(Excerpt)

In renewed, futile attacks between Volga and Don, as well as in Stalingrad, the Soviets suffered high casualties.

23 December 1942
The Last Day in Vassilyevka
Map 15

War Diary of 11th Panzer Regiment

Vassilyevka, 23 Dec 1942

0430hrs.

The night passes quietly except for an enemy attack from the north and northeast at 0345hrs.

0630hrs.

The ordered attack by Hauschild started at 0600hrs. with support from panzers of I/11th Panzer Regiment Simultaneously, Remlinger was attacked by an enemy infantry unit of regimental size with several tanks. But the attack was fended off by our artillery fire. Enemy retreats to Birsovoi.

1200hrs.

During the morning the commanding general [General der Panzertruppen Kirchner] and the division commander [Generalmajor Raus] arrived at the bridgehead to see the situation in person. The attacks by Remlinger and Hauschild are discontinued.

1350hrs.

The order from Division arrived to vacate the bridgehead, as the necessary additional forces are unavailable, making a breakthrough into Stalingrad hopeless. Any further holding of this position also appears to be without purpose, as the flanks are completely unprotected. Moreover, the division can be better used in other areas where the Russians are attempting to break through.

Battle Group Hünersdorff Radio Traffic

0430hrs. Radio Message to Division

Morning Report: Prior to enemy attack from the north and north-east at 0345hrs, the night passed quietly. Ordered procedures in place.

0620hrs. Radio Message to Division
    Attack by Hauschild with panzer support begun at 0600hrs.

0623hrs. Radio Message to Division

Since 0600hrs., enemy infantry attacking with several tanks from the south-east. Remlinger operation must not proceed until after the defence.

0630hrs.

Enemy attack from the south-east halted by our artillery fire. Five enemy tanks return to Birsovoi. From the south, decreasing movements toward Birsovoi.

1345hrs. Radio Message to Division
In area both sides of 117.8, strong enemy position with artillery and anti-tank systems.

1350hrs. Radio Message from Division

Notification: division is to be released tonight and transferred to Potemkinskaya, leaving behind a rear guard. Appropriate preparations to be made. Orders to follow.

In the midst of the effort to expand the bridgehead, and the struggle over starting positions for the further advance toward Stalingrad, the unexpected order arrives to release 6th Panzer Division.

A valid decision, but a difficult one!

The situation on the Donez and at the large bend in the Don river had become so tense and so dangerous to the entire southern front, that the Fourth Panzer Army High Command was ordered to sacrifice three panzer divisions.

It only testifies to the foresight of Generaloberst Hoth, that as commander of Fourth Panzer Army, and fully aware of his own difficult position, he was nevertheless willing to give up his strongest division – the 6th Panzer Division

The Russian armies that faced them included two that had recently become known (the 51st Army and 2nd Guards Army) which had a total of three mechanised corps, one tank corps, three infantry and one cavalry corps. These forces had mostly come from the encirclement at Stalingrad, but there were also new forces among them that had been brought in from the other side of the Volga. Moreover, to offer a comparison using the German military designations (a Russian corps corresponds to one-and-a-half German divisions), two battle-weary German panzer divisions faced 12 enemy divisions.

The Romanian Fourth Army, consisting of two Romanian corps, was assigned to the German Fourth Panzer Army and was tasked with providing flank protection for the German LVII Panzer Corps while it attacked (left to the Don, the Romanian VI Corps, right toward the steppe, the Romanian VII Corps). By this time, the Romanian units could no longer be relied on. Their fighting strength and will to resist had vanished. Sometime later, as there was no alternative, they were returned to their homeland.

The new mission of the 6th Panzer Division was to serve under the XLVIII Panzer Corps. It would replace the 11th Panzer Division on the lower Chir, the division given up by General Hoth. At the Chir, the 6th Panzer Division was to prevent a Russian breach through the now weakened XLVIII Corps.

War Diary of 11th Panzer Regiment

1600hrs.

The order issued to the adjutant by Ia (operations officer) reads as follows:

Expedited departure by 2400hrs., leaving rear guard in place consisting of the panzer regiment, the 6th Reconnaissance Battalion, one company from II/114th Panzer Grenadier Regiment (on SPWs) and two batteries from 76th Artillery Regiment, under the command of Oberst von Hünersdorff.

Destination: Potemkinskaya on the Don.

March Route: 146.9, reception there by 17th Panzer Division, which is stopped in the line of the southern perimeter Solenaya ravine–146.9 to Salivski-Generalovksi to Potemkinskaya.

It had been decided! The Sixth Army had given up its final opportunity to break out, a decision whose rightness or wrongness is easy to judge in retrospect. But who can know of the inner struggles and moral dilemmas of the leaders in that cauldron? As to the extent to which human failure and technical impossibilities informed or dictated the decision, let us not allow ourselves to pass judgment. In recognition of the enormity of this tragedy, the almost unprecedented valour, and the merits of the troops inside as well as out, it is far better to remain silent and bow down before God's judgment.

That the entire basis of the summer offensive and the further development of this assault on Stalingrad and the Caucasus was a mistake is irrefutable. To transfer the blame onto our allies is unjustified. The assessment of their combat strength was a matter for the Wehrmacht high command, and thus also for Hitler, whose ideas served as a basis for the entire operation. These forces should not have been given tasks that, given their low strength, they could never have fulfilled. Moreover, to deploy purely German units only at Voronezh, Stalingrad, and in the Caucasus, and against an enemy like the Russians, was dilettantish. In this manner, the forward units were simply offered up to the Russians for the encirclement. To give due justice to the coalition forces it must be stated that at times, to the extent that was possible given their low strength, the Romanians in particular gave their utmost.

What still remained of the harrowing Stalingrad mission was that we would have to tie up as many Russian forces as possible, for as long as possible, without any hope of reinforcements, in order to enable the southern front of German Army East, which was bleeding from all wounds, to consolidate its position.

24 December 1942

War Diary of 11th Panzer Regiment

Vassilyevka, 24 Dec 1942

0000hrs.

The retreat from the bridgehead begins without enemy interference at 2100hrs. The rear guard disengages at 0000hrs., as ordered, disrupted only by a few fire attacks.

The radio message comes in that the Führer [Hitler] has awarded Oberst von Hünersdorff the Knight's Cross of the Iron Cross.

With this, the first phase of the regiment's battles, an unfortunately futile final attempt to achieve a breakthrough to Stalingrad, now come to an end. The regiment has additional laurels to attach to its colours, and now, undefeated by the enemy, it marches off to new missions.

In radio messages and orders of the day Army Group Don, 4th Panzer Army High Command, and LVII Panzer Corps pay tribute to the performance of 6th Panzer Division, with special recognition to the 11th Panzer Regiment and its commanders.

1800hrs.

At 0500hrs., the last vehicle drives southward across the blocking position formed by 23rd Panzer Division on line 157.0–146.9. Enemy pursuit is weak. At around 1000hrs., after a short refuelling stop, the vehicles cross the bridge in Salivski toward the south. At 1600hrs., they reach Potemkinskaya. Despite initial orders to continue on immediately, the troops are instead allowed to overnight in Potemkinskaya in order rest for the first time since 11 December, and to celebrate Christmas Eve.

Telegram   23 Dec 1942

To the 6th Panzer Division via LVII Panzer Corps

Order of the Day

Tomorrow the 6th Panzer Division is to withdraw from our area of operations. It has borne the main burden of the advance across the Aksai. I wish to express recognition and gratitude of the division, particularly to the 11th Panzer Regiment and its commander for their unswerving fighting spirit, and willingness to make sacrifices.

Hoth
Generaloberst and Commander in
Chief of the 4th Panzer Army

A Related Report
by
Commander, 6/11th Panzer Regiment

The order for our relief, or better said, our separation, found us completely unprepared. Shortly before midnight our panzers, almost the last of the division, left Vassilyevka without enemy interference. In doing so we were vacating one of the points furthest to the east that was still occupied by German Army East at that time. It was already dawn as we drove across our old battlefields, and it was close to midday when we rolled across the bridge in Salivski. Fully replenished with panzers that had been restored in the workshops, we once more had the look of a respectable force. The evening of the 24th found us in Potemkinskaya on the Don.

The village was already filled with Romanians, and we were able to overnight there. After moving into my shelter, I went to find the staff of my battalion, wanting to spend a short time with the commander, Major Dr. Bäke and other comrades on Christmas Eve. Right above me, just as in previous nights, I heard the stream of transport squadrons flying toward Stalingrad. They came from Salsk, as Morosovskaya could no longer be used as a supply base, and even Tatzinskaya had been taken by the enemy. Our future mission was to roll up on these enemy attack vanguards, from the flank outwards, toward the west.

We sat together quietly and pondered the past days as well as the uncertain future. Would the Fourth Panzer Army be able to hold the Aksai without us? Apparently, no one was counting on it, as the present bridge over the Don was to be dismantled immediately after the last vehicle from the 6th Panzer Division had crossed. Would we get out of our present encirclement, which threatened to become much larger than the one at Stalingrad? We placed our faith in the commanders and the strength of our division ...

Wehrmacht Report
24 December 1942

(Excerpt)

Between Volga and Don, 600 prisoners of war captured, and 15 tanks destroyed, counterattacks by the Soviets collapsed.

CHAPTER V

Retrospect and Outlook

December 1942 to January 1943
Map 16

Lessons learned
Assessment of our forces, our allied forces, and those of the enemy
The end situation and later developments
Outside perspectives

The following will be an analysis of the overall situation of the southern front for the period beginning at the end of December 1942, with a short summary of the further developments specifically from perspective of the 6th Panzer Division. A valuable first step, however, would be to take an analytical look at the attack by the Fourth Panzer Army.

Overall, there is little argument as to the necessity of the attack and the manner of its execution, but many factors were in play. With respect to the time of the deployment, it must be stated that by 12 December, it was too late. If this attack had begun on 4 or 5 December according to plan, at a time where the 6th Panzer Division was deployment-ready, the Fourth Panzer Army would have had greater success. On 21 November, the minute the ring closed around Stalingrad, the Wehrmacht High Command should have deployed troops there. For reasons of time and distance, the best choice would have been the divisions and corps of Army Group A in the Caucasus, which were available at that time. In any case, without a stable Don front these divisions would not have been able to continue to hold their positions in the Caucasus.

As understandable as Hitler's order was – never to give up what had been captured – this tactic does not lead to success in battle. No decisive victory can be won without mobility, and without the constant interplay between *Schwerpunkt* (main effort) and risk. This involves giving up ground that is unimportant or cannot be held. Trying to hold onto everything with weak forces simply surrenders the initiative to the enemy.

When it came to Germans and Russians, another factor quickly became apparent: although we were more flexible and superior in leadership, we were always inferior in numbers.

The OKW – the OKH had essentially become too disempowered by this time – should have given up on the situation in the Caucasus with its oil and shifted the entire Army Group A to operational mobility in the area of the Kalmyk steppe and sent it to relieve Stalingrad. Hitler was, however, completely obsessed with his 'hold out to the last' idea, especially because he had undeniably mastered the crisis outside Moscow with this approach during the previous winter. For this reason, he leaves all of Army Group A standing nearly idle, forbids the break-out of the Sixth Army from Stalingrad, and hands over the job of restoring the situation on the Don to Generalfeldmarschall von Manstein, with nothing but wreckage to work with. Then, as if all that had not been enough, he orders Manstein to relieve Stalingrad.

The first of these missions, considering the available forces and the weak and hesitantly led troops, was just about impossible. The second mission, that of relieving Stalingrad, was essential. It therefore remains even more incomprehensible that this mission was ordered without the simultaneous addition of strong troops. This could have been *the* mission for Army Group A. Without any commander in chief – Group A was under the direct command of the Wehrmacht High Command – it remained almost completely in the same old positions, which were much too far away. At the same time, however, it was clear that in case of a breakthrough by the Russians at Rostov, not only would this army group be cut off, but the oil – as Hitler repeatedly pointed out – could not be transported out of the area.

It was almost a miracle that at this moment, the 6th Panzer Division was so readily available. It was brought in by rail from Brittany beginning in early November, that is, before the surrounding of Stalingrad, to serve as reserves behind the Italian Army on the Don. This was a sound move, but 'too late' again: by the time they arrived, the crisis had greatly expanded. Instead of receiving the needed forces from the Caucasus, the newly forming Fourth Panzer Army received only the LVII General Headquarters (corps headquarters), and the worn-down 23rd Panzer Division. By giving up the bend of the Terek river, the fully intact 16th Infantry Division (motorised) which had only been tying down enemy forces, could have been released and supplied to the Fourth Army. Furthermore, other forces from Army Group Don could have been provided for the benefit of Army Group A. The promised 15th Luftwaffe Field Division not only had limited attack power, but was still not completely put together, and in any case, it arrived too late. Precious hours were squandered before the Wehrmacht High Command finally realised this and sent in the 17th Panzer Division, stationed at Orel, as reserves. But the delayed decision caused this unit, too, to arrive on the battlefield too late.

These three German divisions alone – the Romanians no longer counted as an attack force – might well have been too weak to relieve Stalingrad under any circumstances. Yet there was still hope, and not a totally foolish one, of still being able to rescue the surrounded troops. This would involve two spearhead attacks: the XLVIII Panzer Corps, which was still in need of reinforcements, would attack from the Chir bridgehead, and simultaneously, the Sixth Army would break out of the encirclement.

How could this well-formulated intent be transformed into action considering the following realities?

1) The XLVIII Panzer Corps did not receive the expected divisions, because these were, if they arrived at all, deployed at crisis locations, with the result that the corps had been robbed of its attack power; it could only hold its positions with the greatest of effort. It could not recapture Kalach, an important Don bridge, nor could it hold the bridgehead at the Chir mouth. For that corps the only task remaining was to tie down Russian forces.

2) The LVII Panzer Corps did receive its expected divisions, but because the 23rd Panzer Division had to leave its wheeled vehicles behind due to the thawing period on the steppe, it arrived too late. Instead of the more

favourable time of early December, the attack could not begin until 12 December. The 17th Panzer Division, for the above-mentioned reasons, participated only in the second half of the attack which was already in progress. One can well imagine the degree of success that might have been granted the LVII Panzer Corps had it been able to command the 17th Panzer Division from the very start of the attack. Had this been the case, the delayed attack date would have been well compensated by strength.

3) The Sixth Army could not commit itself to breaking out, so that the entire operation plan to set them free essentially collapsed: the forces outside were too weak to break through the ring alone.

Above all, the season proved unfavourable for large operations. The days were much too short and often prevented a budding victory to reach full bloom. It was not until later that the chance for a victory on the steppe presented itself, despite the disconnected fronts, and the darkness of night. But the successful advance on Vassilyevka was not founded completely on the boldness of Battle Group Hünersdorff, but on a bit of good fortune involving the failure of the Russian intelligence technology. The earlier successful breach of the enemy's strong anti-tank gun positions at Hill 146.9 proved that the night can become a great aid to the attacker. Although it may be presumptuous to draw generalised theories from one attack by the LVII Panzer Corps, the fact remains that because of the German Wehrmacht's fear of engaging in night attacks, which was later more or less discarded, many chances for victory had been wasted.

For scheduled movements, the iced-over ravines (*Balkas*) not only disrupted and impeded our progress, but also had an effect on our decisions and successes (Chilekov on 12/13, Askai bridge at Salivski on 13, 14, 15, and 16 December and at Nekliksaya ravine on 17 December). Depending on temperatures, by day or by night, these presented a difficult hazard. On the slick surfaces, especially if the thermometer read over zero, or if a short period of sunshine had thawed the southern slope, neither snow chains on the wheeled vehicles, nor ice studs for the panzers, were of any help. The panzers spun down the slopes as if on a tilted sheet of ice. In the fluctuating temperatures, the more traffic on the roads leading through the ravines, the slicker the surfaces. When short bursts of sun rays appeared, followed quickly by frost, all the work done by the pioneers – deployed here for this very reason – was quickly cancelled out.

Added to this was the delay in the urgently needed bridge construction at the Aksai in Salivski. Due to inability to bring in ammunition and fuel, those troops who had fought from the beginning were deprived of success. It had come to this, even though every panzer always carried almost double the expected amount of ammunition needed (for instance the Panzer III 5cm long: about 200 rounds and 5,000 to 7,000 rounds of machine gun ammunition).

The issue of carrying ammunition and fuel along vs. having it re-supplied deserves some serious discussion. Measures taken by the troops on their own initiative proved to be temporary and were limited to specific vehicle types, regions, or other particulars.

In quickly shifting situations a stricter leadership is needed when it comes to coded radio messages. A critical appraisal of the radio messages quoted in this book reveals again and again that the radio orders from the division often no longer fit the situation. Due to technical difficulties, answers to questions were delayed. This meant that they reached the commanders too late, and the decisions that came from them were no longer valid ones. This presents a definite obstacle to rapid mobile operations! The encoding regulations and the way they were used by the German army during the war made it impossible to quickly summarise a situation and develop a *Schwerpunkt* – the most important basic principle in leading an attack by a panzer division. Although concrete proposals for changes in this area are beyond the purpose of this work, the documentary evidence in the reports quoted here demonstrates that even within the structure of division-level leadership (in lower echelons, below the level of battalion or section, radio messages were not encoded), a faster means of conveying orders must be found.

It is left to us to commemorate the achievements of the troops on both sides of the encirclement. It is true that the larger goal of rescuing the troops there provided us all with a special incentive, but the fighting spirit of the grenadiers, panzer crews and the other military branches deserves special recognition, having suffered through the cold weather and faced a tough, numerically superior enemy. The re-supply units, despite the rough terrain and the vast areas that were under enemy fire, constantly tried to bring ammunition, fuel and provisions to the comrades fighting at the front – sometimes unsuccessfully, but through no fault of their own. The workshops and the repair services worked without respite. No one let his comrades down.

The cooperation in the corps down to the smallest units and battle groups was outstanding. In the case of the older, more seasoned divisions, it once more became evident how important it was to know and trust one another. For this reason alone, they were far superior in comparison to the newly established units. Unfortunately, as the war drew to its close, the highest levels of leadership failed to recognise this fact. Increasingly, the old divisions with tried-and-true troops were permitted to bleed dry, while we searched for salvation in the multitude of newly established units. We often paid for this with blood. As late as 1945, the exhausted, but more experienced divisions had far more defensive victories than the newly established ones that were equally well-equipped. Experience can neither be taught nor learned but gathered by the individual over the course of time.

As to our enemy in the Kalmyk steppe, one cannot deny him respect. He may have fought differently, but he never lacked in fighting spirit, toughness, or ruthlessness toward himself. In these areas we can only continue to learn from him. He, too, knew what was at stake. The errors in leadership, which could clearly be seen at the time, cannot be analysed in detail until such time as appropriate documentation is available from his side.

In particular, the Romanians showed themselves to be excellent soldiers, especially those who later fought under German leadership. In toughness and fearlessness for their own lives, they were similar to the Russians. Their own commanders may have been of lesser quality, and to be fair, their equipment was not equal to that of the enemy. Moreover, there was no relationship of trust and loyalty between commanders and subordinates. Symptomatic of this was the fact that in a Romanian company, there were separate messes (very different from one another!) for officers, NCOs, and soldiers.

End Situation and Assessment

At the end of December 1942, the situation between Voroshilovgrad and the Kalmyk steppe had deteriorated to the point that it was not only about the encircled troops, but also about the fate of the entire German Southern Front.

At this point, the Russians had only been held at bay by small, scattered German units, particularly Group Fretter-Pico in the area of Millerovo, which held on tenaciously amid heavy losses. The Russians were now positioned in Tatzinskaya, in the centre of the large bend in the Don river in the outskirts of Morosovskaya, deep in the rear of the German troops fighting at the Chir river. They were now pushing harder in the direction of the important Donez bridges.

The Fourth Panzer Army stood south of the Don, and after the departure of the 6th Panzer Division, had only had two weak German divisions. Unable to hold back the heavy Russian counterattack on 25 December, they had to retreat by way of the old starting positions at Kotelnikovo to an area behind the Sal river. Without flank security, the Russians could repeatedly raid their positions using double envelopments out in the vast, open steppe. In mid-January the Fourth Army was able to link up with Army Group A, which was also retreating. They were reinforced by the relatively strong 16th Infantry Division (motorised), which came from Elista. Only then did Fourth Panzer Army finally gain a somewhat firm position on the Manych river.

When the Fourth Panzer Army retreated (it was weaker than a corps in terms of size), the Russians took advantage of the opportunity and crossed the Don at Potemkinskaya and Zymlyanksaya. They then attacked the troops in the rear that were fighting at the Chir river (Army Detachment Hollidt and XLVIII Panzer Corps). The 6th Panzer Division was attached to these units but had already crossed over the Don. For the units left behind at the Chir, their only option was to secure the rear of the quickly organised Group Mieth and relocate to Tatzinskaya on the Donez, via Morosovskaya.

The retreat took place between 27 Dec 1942 and 20 Jan 1943. There was no sense of panic, but as the units moved back, they also counterattacked, often inflicting heavy casualties on the Russians.

Back in mid-December 1942, the Italian Army had dropped out. Now, the Hungarian Army south of Voronezh failed completely, creating a similar crisis. But Army Group Don was able to hold the Donez, and by springtime of 1943, after heavy fighting, the new situation was brought back under control and was finalised with the recapture of Kharkov.

It is unfortunate that currently there are no translations available of archived reports on the German advance to relieve Stalingrad.

The following excerpts from Russian, English, and Romanian publications, however, attest to how significant the battles in the Kalmyk steppe were for the Russians, as well as for the Germans.

The numbers cited in these works are mostly inaccurate, particularly those in the Malinovki report, which are subject to bias and are likely much exaggerated. From these documents, however, the reader is free to form his or her own impressions.

The Soviet Land
The Great War of the Fatherland of the Soviet Union 1917–1947
I. I. Mine, I. M. Rasgon and A. L. Sidorow
SWA-Verlag, Berlin 1947
Pages 104–5:

> Simultaneously the Soviet units contained the attack by the Manstein Group, which had attempted to break through from Kotelnikov to Stalingrad. In bitter defensive fighting they allowed the enemy to bleed out and, after reinforcements had arrived, transitioned to attack mode. The Manstein Group suffered a decisive defeat.

> All possibility of rescuing the encircled troops was now beyond the reach of the German High Command …

Sowjetmarschälle haben das Wort (*Soviet Marshals Have Their Say*)
Kyrill D. Kalinov
Hansa-Verlag Josef Toth, Hamburg 1950
Pages 285–287:

> Malinovski begins his presentation with this:

On 11 December 1942 we intercepted a message addressed to Paulus which was worded as follows: 'Begin morning offensive to liberate you. Orders from the Führer. Counting on celebrating Christmas with you.'[1]

In fact, on 12 December the German offensive did begin. The starting point was Tsimlianskaya. Von Manstein had prepared considerable troops: four armoured divisions (6th, 11th, 17th, and 24th), two motorised divisions (15th and 16th), three infantry divisions (4th, 5th, and 18th), two divisions of Romanian cavalry, twelve artillery regiments, as well as an independent air fleet. The entirety formed a 'mot pulk', consisting of the best forces in the Wehrmacht.[i] Its firepower in cannons and panzers was fully equal to our forces against which the attack was directed.

The first days saw extremely hard fighting. The Germans succeeded in crossing the Aksai and pushing through onto the left bank of the Don as far as the small river Chir, and on the right bank as far as Abganorovo.

We had to request our heavy tanks and our anti-tank guns in order to bring von Manstein to a halt. Besides these, our combat aviation units, our Yaks, our Migs and our Laggs, had to be brought in as quickly as possible.

The 16th of December, the decisive day, arrived. The Germans drew nearer to Stalingrad, coming as close as just 42km from the ring. The German soldiers trapped inside the city could hear the thunder of the cannons in the distance.

On 17 and 18 December we deployed all of our available tanks against von Manstein's panzers. Yeremenko even gave the order to send the 1,500 tanks that were being held in reserve by the high command to the most threatened place in the sector, the village of Biriukov. Vassilievski protested this measure. But after a short quarrel over who had the direct authority for this, Stalin permitted Yeremenko's measures.

The tank battle near the village of Biriukov developed in to one of the most difficult of the entire war. Against the 1,000 German panzers, we sent double the number into the battle. The entire success of our operations at Stalingrad was at risk if we did not succeed in intercepting the Germans here. No cost was too high.

Meanwhile, I requested permission from Voronov to send the 3,000 motorised guns, which he held in reserve, to the 42km wide corridor, which still separated von Manstein from the Paulus army. On 21 December these batteries opened

---

i   *Mot pulk* = a particular type of motorised formation attributed to the Germans in World War II.

fire from all tubes. The effect was so powerful that after three days von Manstein only had 400 panzers and two artillery regiments left. The armoured part of the 'mot pulk' formation was completely in shreds.

Then on 24 December we transitioned to the offensive.

Over the next three days we threw von Manstein not just back to his starting positions, but also forced him to retreat even further. In the process of pursuit, my army captured the village of Kotelnikovo.

Stalingrad
Steinberg-Verlag, Zürich 1945
The first authentic report of the Russian Generals Rokossovski, Voronov, Telegin, Malinin, and war correspondents about one of the largest and most decisive battles in world history.
Pages 15–16:

After the German high command had led its troops into a blind alley in the outskirts of Stalingrad, and delivered them into a catastrophic situation, it undertook the desperate attempt to liberate its troops encircled by the Red Army at Stalingrad. To this purpose, the enemy concentrated a strong assembly of troops in the area north of Kotelnikovo, and on 12 December, began its attack operations against our troops.

The Soviet troops, which operated south of Stalingrad, were tasked by the high command of the Red Army to defeat enemy's new assault group, push the Germans back toward the south, and remove all possibility of their reaching the divisions trapped in Stalingrad…

In the attacks in the area south of Stalingrad, the Soviet troops advanced 100 to 150km and liberated more than 130 villages. During the battles from 12 through 30 December, the Soviet troops defeated: the German 6th, 17th, and 23rd Panzer Divisions, and the 16th Motorised Division, and the Romanian 4th and 18th Infantry, and 5th and 18th Cavalry Divisions. The deaths alone cost the German Fascists 21,000 men. The number of captured came to 5,200 soldiers and officers. Included in the wealth of captured goods brought in by the Soviet troops were: 40 aircraft, 94 panzers, 292 cannons, 329 motor vehicles and a large quantity of other weapons, as well as military equipment related to the air force and panzer forces.

In the battles, the Soviet troops destroyed: 306 aircraft, 667 panzers, 257 cannons, 945 motor vehicles, and many other kinds of military goods.

Ibid, pages 58 and 59:

> During the process of encirclement, the Soviet high command immediately secured the units that were surrounding the enemy in the west, south-west and south. Some of this security force held back the advance by Manstein in tough fighting.
>
> But then our glorious guards' divisions broke out like an avalanche from the north toward the south, pushed back Manstein's panzer units, took Kotelnikovo, and pushed the entire Group Don to Rostov.
>
> The hopes of the encircled Fascists for the defeat of our troops had vanished, and with them went the hopes for their liberation…

> (Michail Bragin)

The Hinge of Fate
Winston S. Churchill
Alfred Scherz Verlag, Bern 1951, page 637; English edition, Houghton Mifflin, Boston, 1951, page 734:

> We must now revert to the tremendous drama unfolding around Stalingrad. As has been described, Paulus's Sixth German Army had been caught by the Russian pincers and encircled as the result of the November conflict. Manstein's supreme effort from the south-west in December to break through the Russian cordon and relieve the beleaguered garrison had failed. He pierced the Russian line to a depth of forty miles, but there he was stopped, still fifty miles from Stalingrad. A new Russian offensive from the north threatened his flank and forced him into a retreat which spread to all the German southern front, including the Causasus, and ended only when it was back behind Rostov-on-the-Don.
>
> There was now no hope of further succour for Paulus.

Der zweite Weltkrieg 1939–1945 (*World War II 1939–1945*)
General-Major J. F. C. Fuller
Humboldt-Verlag, Wien-Stuttgart 1950
Pages 298 and 299:

> After von Manstein had assembled an army with the strength of about 150,000 men, he advanced to the railway line Salsk-Stalingrad, broke through the Russian lines between Tsimlyansk and Kotelnikovo; after a tough battle, he captured the second of these villages. Yet hardly had this happened, when, on the 16th Valutin attacked Bokovsk in the north of his left flank. General Golikov's army group, which now appeared at Valutin's right, took Boguchar on Don and overran

the Italian Eighth Army. Because of this upheaval, Manstein's left flank and the area that lay to his rear, was now exposed. The reserves that were allocated for his front were quickly sent to the north, so as to stop Valutin's advance, and that of Golikov on Millerovo, a station on the extremely important railway line Voronezh-Rostov. This scattering of reserves led, at least partially, to the defeat of Manstein's right flank. Here, on the 27th, he was defeated by the tank forces of General Malinovski, which is also why Kotelnikovo was lost. For the relief army, this meant failure.

Rumäniens Weg zum Satellitenstaat (Romania's Path to Becoming a Satellite Country)
Jon Gheorghe
Kurt Vowinckel Verlag, Heidelberg 1952
Pages 269–70:

> Left and right of Stalingrad there are enormous, gaping holes. The German Sixth Army and the Romanian troops that had been forced back toward them, were in a bind.
>
> Now the German commanders stood before a new, difficult question of a strategic and psychological sort: Stalingrad had become a symbol of the battle in the east, and in fact for Germany itself, as well as for the Soviets. Strategic wisdom required that the Sixth Army and the significant amount of war materiel be rescued. But the German commanders gave precedence to the psychological aspect. Stalingrad had to be held for reasons of prestige and had to be relieved. The German commanders believed that the connection to the encirclement could be restored through rash, improvised measures. They appointed Feldmarschall von Manstein and awarded him the command of all the German-Romanian forces. Many had become exhausted, but then fresh troops were thrown in head over heels. From all corners, even from France, significant forces rolled in, above all panzer units. They assembled in the area of Rostov, as Manstein's mission did not only consist of consolidating the fronts and relieving Stalingrad, but it was also a matter of securing the troops operating in the Caucasus and holding the route open to Rostov. Some of Manstein's undertakings showed, at least in initial their initial approach, a splendid personal character. This was primarily apparent in the south-west of Stalingrad, where two newly arrived panzer divisions, with support from Romanian forces, advanced nearer to Stalingrad. The superiority of the German troops proved clear, but their numbers were unfortunately too small. Despite splendid successes in the beginning, they were not able to cope with the onrush of Bolshevik masses. Now Manstein had to limit himself to halting the Russian assault in order to secure the important traffic hub of Rostov.

Index of Names of Commanders, Adjutants, and Company Commanders

(As of 12 December 1942)

Fourth Panzer Army	Generaloberst Hoth
I/VII Panzer Corps	General der Panzertruppen Kirchner
Chief of General Staff	Oberst i. G. Laegeler (i.G. = on the General Staff)
6th Panzer Division	Generalmajor Raus
17th Panzer Division	Generalleutnant von Senger and Etterlin
23rd Panzer Division	Generaleutnant Freiherr von Boineburg-Lengsfeld

6th Panzer Division

Commander	General Raus
1a Operations	Oberstleutnant von Kassell
1b Second General Staff Officer	Hauptmann Schreiber
Ic Chief Intelligence Officer	Hauptmann Dr. Erdmann
01 First Assistant Adjutant	Oberleutnant Müller
IIa Division Adjutant	Hauptmann Poche

4th Panzer Grenadier Regiment

Commander	Oberst Unrein
Adjutant	Oberleutnant Graf v. u. z. Hoensbroech (Ignaz)[i]

I Battalion

Commander	Rittmeister Remlinger
Adjutant	Oberleutnant Lehmann
1st Company	Oberleutnant Fröhlich
2nd Company	Oberleutnant Donner
3rd Company	Oberleutnant Graf v. u. z. Hoensbroech (Franz)
4th Company	Oberleutnant Bachmann

II Battalion

Commander	Hauptmann Kreis
Adjutant	Leutnant Reinecke
5th Company	Oberleutnant Bake
6th Company	Oberleutnant Reimar
7th Company	Oberleutnant Herwig
8th Company	Oberleutnant Müller
9th Company	Hauptmann Jürgensmeyer

114th Panzer Grenadier Regiment

Commander	Oberst Zollenkopf
Adjutant	Oberleutnant Stöcker

I Battalion

Commander	Major Hauschild
Adjutant	Leutnant Timmer
1st Company	Oberleutnant Hertmanni
2nd Company	Oberleutnant Jung
3rd Company	Oberleutnant Kleinmann
4th Company	Oberleutnant Kelletat

---

i   v. u. z. = *von und zu* , initials used with some names of noble families.

II Battalion (SPW)

Commander	Hauptmann Küper
Adjutant	Oberleutnant Jaeger
5th Company	Oberleutnant Koch
6th Company	Oberleutnant Schäfer
7th Company	Oberleutnant Roembke
8th Company	Oberleutnant Badzuweit
9th Company	Oberleutnant Vallbracht

11th Panzer Regiment

Commander	Oberst von Hünersdorff
Adjutant	Oberleutnant Ritgen

1st Battalion

Commander	Major Löwe
Adjutant	Oberleutnant te Heesen
1st Company	Hauptmann Hoffmeyer
2nd Company	Hauptmann Hagemeister
3rd Company	Oberleutnant Scharfe
4th Company	Hauptmann Wils

II Battalion

Commander	Major Dr. Bäke
Adjutant	Oberleutnant Guckel
5th Company	Oberleutnant Sander
6th Company	Oberleutnant Scheibert
7th Company	Oberleutnant Ranzinger

76th Panzer Artillery Regiment

Commander	Oberst von Grundherr
Adjutant	Hauptmann Klapper

I Battalion

Commander	Major Schulz
Adjutant	Oberleutnant Kesseler

1st Battery	Oberleutnant Sauerborn
2nd Battery	Hauptmann Bering
3rd Battery	Hauptmann Jahn

II Battalion

Commander	Hauptmann Blecher
Adjutant	Oberleutnant Sachse
4th Battery	Oberleutnant Kost
5th Battery	Hauptmann Hacke
6th Battery	Oberleutnant Neuhaus

III Battalion

Commander	Major Graf
Adjutant	Oberleutnant Bauch
7th Battery	Oberleutnant Grimm
8th Battery	Hauptmann Hölzer
9th Battery	Oberleutnant Plecher

6th Panzer Reconnaissance Battalion

Commander	Major Quentin
Adjutant	Oberleutnant Grothe
1st Company	Oberleutnant Bockhoff
2nd Company	Oberleutnant Wisemann
3rd Company	Oberleutnant Walthermate
4th Company	Oberleutnant Fricke
5th Company	Hauptmann Jonas

41st Panzerjäger Battalion

Commander	Hauptmann Neckenauer
Adjutant	Oberleutnant Dr. Timm
1st Company	Oberleutnant Durban
2nd Company	Oberleutnant Schön
3rd Company (*Flak*)	Oberleutnant Wengenrot

LVII Panzer Pioneer Battalion

Commander	Major Wolff
Adjutant	Oberleutnant Böckmann
1st Company	Oberleutnant Rösener
2nd Company	Oberleutnant Prinz
3rd Company	Hauptmann Andersch
Light Pioneer Company	Hauptmann Thuy

82nd Panzer Intelligence Battalion

Commander	Major Dr. Schauer
Adjutant	Leutnant Moll
1st Company	Oberleutnant Gödde
2nd Company	Oberleutnant Uckel
Light Column	Hauptmann Müller

Bibliography

Churchill, W. S., *Memoiren*, Band 4, Buch 2, Bern 1951.

Fuller, J. F. Ch., *Der zweite Weltkrieg*, Stuttgart 1950.

Gheorghe, J., *Rumäniens Weg zum Satellitenstaat*, Heidelberg 1952.

Kalinov, Kyrill D., *Sowjetmarschälle haben das Wort*, Hamburg 1950.

Kern, Erich, *Buch der Tapferkeit*, Druffel-Verlag 1953.

v. Manstein, Erich, *Verlorene Siege*, Bad Godesberg-Bonn 1955.

Matello, H. H., 'Versammlung und Vorstoß der 6. deutschen Panzer Division zur Befreiung von Stalingrad,' Schweizer Militärschrift, Jg.116, Nr. 6, 7, 8, 1950.

Michel, Karl, *Es begann am Don*, Bern 1946.

Mine, I. I., *Der große vaterländische Krieg der Sovjetunion*, Berlin, SWA-Verlag 1947.

Ritgen, Helmut, 'Durchbruch nach Bol.-Wassiljewka am 19 Dec 1942,' in *Die Panzertruppe*, Juni 1943.

v. Rohden, Herhudt, *Die Luftwaffe ringt um Stalingrad*, Wiesbaden 1950.

Scheibert, Justus, *7 Jahre unter Rebellen*.

Schröter, Heinz, *Stalingrad ... bis zur letzten Patrone*, Osnabrück 1953.

v. Schulz, Joachim, *Zum Gedächtnis an General Helmuth v. Pannwitz, dem obersten Feldataman der Kosaken*, Geopolitik 1953.

Selle, H., *Die Tragödie von Stalingrad*, Hannover 1948.

Stalin, I. V., *Über den großen vaterländischen Krieg der Sowjetunion*, Moskau 1946.

Stalingrad, *Die ersten Berichte der russischen Generale*, Zürich 1945.

Toepke, G., *Stalingrad, wie es wirklich war*, Stade 1949.

Journals and other sources

OKW Berichte (Wehrmacht High Command reports).

Kriegstagebuch Panzerregiment 11 (War Diary of 11th Panzer Regiment).

Kriegstagebuch des Verfassers (War Diary of author).

Kriegstagebuch 'Spähtrupp Diepenbrock', Aufklärungs Abteilung 6 (Journal of Scout Troop Diepenbrock, VI Reconnaissance Battalion).

Funksprüche des Panzer Regiment 11, (11th Panzer Regiment radio messages) in possession of the then Regimental Adjutant Helmut Ritgen.

Endnotes

Introduction

1   Athenäum-Verlag, Bad Godesberg-Bonn 1955, 130.

Chapter I

1   Erich von Manstein, *Verlorene Siege*, Bad Godesberg-Bonn, 1955.

Chapter II

1   Colonel von Pannwitz, later Oberster Feldstaman of the Cossacks.
2   Central European time; local time in Stalingrad area is about two hours later.
3   Brackets […] are author's additions, not found in the original.
4   Later commander of the heavy Panzer Regiment Bäke; see: N. v. Vormann, *Der Kessell von Tcherkassy* (*Die Wehrmacht im Kampf*, Band 3), Heidelberg 1954 [English translation: N. von Vormann (trans. Geoffrey Brooks), *The Battle of Korsun-Cherkassy* (Havertown, Pa: Casemate, 2019)].
5   Later commander of the 505th Tiger Battalion. See: O. Heidkämper, *Witebsk-Kampft und Untergang der 3. Panzerarmee* (*Die Wehrmacht im Kampf*, Band 1) Heidelberg 1954 [English translation: O. Heidkämper (trans. Linden Lyons), Vitebsk (Havertown, Pa: Casemate, 2017)].
6   All time references in these orders are given in local time.
7   This map, which was not available to the German side, designates areas that are either unknown or are spelled somewhat differently.
8   The name *Aksai* will here and in future refer to the river Kurmoyarski-Aksai that flows through Kotelnikovo.
9   II Battalion/14th Panzer Grenadier Regiment (mechanised).

Chapter III

1   Commander of 4th Panzer Grenadier Regiment.
2   No longer available.
3   E. v. Manstein, *Verlorene Siege.*
4   See page 41.
5   See page 42.
6   E. v. Manstein, *Verlorene Siege*, with author's permission.
7   West of the Don.
8   A first allocation of supplies covers about three days of battle.

Chapter IV

1   From 12 to 24 December, the War Diary of the 11th Panzer Regiment and The War Diary of Battle Group Hünersdorff will be the same.
2   Here and later, this refers to 'Jessoulovski-Aksai'.
3   Major Justus Scheibert, *7 Monate in den Rebellenstaaten.*
4   For his company (6/11th Panzer Regiment), the author needed slightly over five hours during this night to get all of his panzers through the gulch.
5   An advance by the 16th Motorised Infantry Division out of Elista.
6   Sub-groups of Battle Group Hünersdorff.
7   Same as above.
8   It only attacked 6th Company, which was under command of this author.
9   Report from the platoon leader, see further on.
10   Later, 36 destroyed tanks were found in this area.
11   It is not completely clear what this message is referring to. (Possibly refers to message that came in at 0730 hrs.)
12   As it later turned out, this message was never sent by Löwe. It was therefore assumed that this was a case of deliberate radio interference by the Russians.
13   Only for 11th Panzer Regiment.
14   Dead.
15   Combat ready: 6 Panzer IIs, 21 Panzer IIIs (5cm, long), 7 Panzer IIIs (7.5cm, short), 5 Panzer IVs (7.5cm, long), 2 command panzers.
16   Code name for certain terrain points.
17   Shortly afterwards these tanks proved to be the same ones already destroyed on 14 December.
18   *Fliegerverbindungsoffizier* = forward air controller, Air Liaison Officer.
19   A B C D were code designations for certain terrain points.
20   Oberst von Hünersdorff began his career in the 4th Hussars Regiment.
21   E. v. Manstein, *Verlorene Siege.*
22   Both from the book: *Verlorene Siege*, E. v. Manstein, quoted here with the kind permission of the author.

23 Verkhne Kumski.

24 Located at the Myshkova, north of Verkhne Kumski, 10km west of Gromoslavka.

25 Code word for break-out of Sixth Army in the direction of Chir bridgehead.

26 Major Dr. Bäke came to his own decision and also allowed some panzers on the southern bank to prevent the loss of the important bridges.

27 Four panzers (5cm, long), two Panzer IIIs (7.5cm, short) and one command panzer (*Befehlspanzer*).

28 E. v. Manstein, *Verlorene Siege*.

29 Actually, only the 5th Company/11th Panzer Regiment.

Chapter V

1 This order was never issued!

Index